Praise for
The Heaven Promise

"I'm genuinely excited by *The Heaven Promise*. With so many fascinated by the conversation of heaven and even near-death experiences, McKnight calls us to see heaven through the lens of Scripture and the redemption story of God in Christ. It's both theologically robust and very accessible. This book speaks to pastors and leaders in the church as well as to parishioners in the pews. What a gift!"

—REV. EUGENE CHO, senior pastor, Quest Church, and author of
Overrated: Are We More in Love with the Idea of Changing the World Than Actually Changing the World?

"This book—grounded in solid research and biblical interpretation—actually stirs up a longing for heaven. It's a busting up of stereotypes and misconceptions. Thank you, Scot McKnight, for painting a picture of a place I would actually love to be for eternity!"

—NANCY BEACH, leadership coach with Slingshot Group, and author
of *Gifted to Lead: The Art of Leading as a Woman in the Church*

"What a terrific book! Scot lays out the great questions about heaven—What will it be like? Who's going there?—and seeks to address them with biblically grounded wisdom."

—JOHN ORTBERG, senior pastor, Menlo Park Presbyterian Church, and
author of *All the Places to Go*

"Fanciful visions and imaginative opinions of heaven are all around us. Thankfully Scot McKnight moves us beyond the realm of wishes to the great promise of heaven given us by God. With wit, care, and fine biblical insight, this book offers a clear understanding of the hope we have for life with God in a heavenly kingdom far better than we can imagine. *The Heaven Promise* is a gift to the church."

—VINCENT BACOTE, PHD, director, Center for Applied Christian
Ethics, Wheaton College

"I serve in a community where hopelessness and resilience coexist and the constant reality of death looms daily. Hope and clarity about heaven's promise are truly needed to empower the church, especially among those most affected by these realities. Scot McKnight helps the church to realize God's truth about the life to come. This brings hope for us in the now."

—PASTOR PHIL JACKSON, MDIV, associate pastor of Lawndale
Christian Community Church; lead pastor of The House,
Christ-Centered Hip-Hop Worship Service; and founder and
chief visionary officer of the Firehouse Community Art Center

"Scot McKnight's timely words help us understand the importance of God's Heaven Promise at a time when the world—and the church—is reeling from one tragedy after another. His biblical approach firmly grounds the imagination, reminding us that God is All in All. I agree with Scot that everything hinges on the resurrection of Jesus, and that means not only the heaven to come, but also the way heaven people live now. We cannot know everything about heaven now, but what we can understand makes us want to say with the apostle John, 'Amen. Come, Lord Jesus!'"

—DR. KENT BRANTLY, Ebola survivor and co-author of *Called for Life*

THE
HEAVEN
PROMISE

Books by Scot McKnight

The Jesus Creed: Loving God, Loving Others

Embracing Grace: Discovering the Gospel that Restores Us to God, Creation, and Ourselves

Praying with the Church: Following Jesus Daily, Hourly, Today

The Blue Parakeet: Rethinking How You Read the Bible

Fasting

One Life: Jesus Calls, We Follow

The King Jesus Gospel: The Original Good News Revisited

Kingdom Conspiracy: Returning to the Radical Mission of the Local Church

A Fellowship of Differents: Showing the World God's Design for Life Together

*Engaging the Bible's Truth
About Life to Come*

THE
HEAVEN
PROMISE

SCOT McKNIGHT

WATERBROOK
PRESS

THE HEAVEN PROMISE
PUBLISHED BY WATERBROOK PRESS
12265 Oracle Boulevard, Suite 200
Colorado Springs, Colorado 80921

Italics in Scripture quotations reflect the author's added emphasis.

Details in some anecdotes and stories have been changed to protect the identities of the persons involved.

Hardcover ISBN 978-1-60142-628-4
eBook ISBN 978-1-60142-630-7

Cover design by Kristopher K. Orr

Published in the United States by WaterBrook Multnomah, an imprint of the Crown Publishing Group, a division of Penguin Random House LLC, New York.

WATERBROOK and its deer colophon are registered trademarks of Penguin Random House LLC.

Excerpts in Chapter 14 are taken from *Forgiving Our Fathers and Mothers: Finding Freedom from Hurt and Hate* by Leslie Leyland Fields and Dr. Jill Hubbard. Copyright © 2014 by Leslie Fields and Dr. Jill Hubbard. Used by permission of Thomas Nelson. www.thomasnelson.com. All rights reserved.

Library of Congress Cataloging-in-Publication Data
McKnight, Scot.
    The heaven promise : engaging the Bible's truth about life to come / Scot McKnight—First Edition.
        pages cm
    Includes bibliographical references.
    ISBN 978-1-60142-628-4—ISBN 978-1-60142-630-7 (electronic) 1. Heaven—Christianity. I. Title.
    BT846.3.M348 2015
    236'.24—dc23
                                        2015017200

Printed in the United States of America
2015—First Edition

10 9 8 7 6 5 4 3 2 1

For my aging parents:
Alex and Lois McKnight,
who think about Heaven

Grant us, Lord, not to be anxious about earthly things, but to love things heavenly; and even now, while we are placed among things that are passing away, to hold fast to those that shall endure; through Jesus Christ our Lord, who lives and reigns with you and the Holy Spirit, one God, for ever and ever. Amen.

—THE BOOK OF COMMON PRAYER

Contents

Part 4: Ten Questions About Heaven

Part One

THE HEAVEN QUESTION

Visit a local bookshop or Google "heaven," and you will quickly discover that heaven is an intense human-interest story. In fact, a shelf or two of books about heaven are published each year. Add to these the stories of near-death experiences, and we have the makings of Hollywood movies about heaven.

Many are asking what I call The Heaven Question: Is there a heaven after we die or not? That question, of course, leads to others, such as: Who will be there? Will I be there? What will heaven be like?

But others are asking an entirely different question: Shouldn't we be focusing on life now and living for the kingdom now and making the kingdom more of a reality now?

That question must be answered with a firm yes, but before we move on, we have to get a stronger grip on what the Bible means by the word *heaven*. Once we do, not only can we be firm in our yes, but we can also learn how Heaven people ought to live today.

Talk about heaven excites the imagination of many people, some of whom just might surprise you.

Surprising Places

Some Children, an Atheist, Authors, a Movie Star, and Questions

> Guesses, of course, only guesses. If they are not true,
> something better will be.
>
> — C. S. Lewis

Even in a world where religious faith is in decline, when someone asks, "Is there a heaven?" most people have an answer or at least a guess. Some are astonishingly bold about what they think heaven will be like and who will be there. We often hear responses that surprise us. Children, for instance, often think about heaven.

When I was a child, I asked my mother if something I liked at that time would be in heaven. Her response was simple and memorable: "If it will make you happy, it will be in heaven." Little did I know she had something up her sleeve with the word "happy."

One Sunday, sitting in the front row at church (and for some reason my mother was next to me and not in the choir loft), the pastor, who had taken up golf, said, "I have learned to enjoy golf, but I wonder if there will be room in heaven for golf." Afterward I said to Mother, "I know there will be golf in heaven." She asked, "How do you know that?" I responded, "Because it will make me happy."

She gave me the kind of look that indicated that the pastor was probably right and that I should retool my sense of what I needed to make me happy.

When that great theologian and Christian martyr Dietrich Bonhoeffer and his twin sister Sabine were children, they nightly put themselves to sleep pondering the word *eternity*. World War I was in motion; Bonhoeffer's oldest brother, Walter, died in that war; and his mother was staggered by Walter's death. Death filled their not particularly religious home. Bonhoeffer later admitted that he could be obsessed with dying a good death. To cope with his fears—and amid the phosphorescent crosses that gleamed in their room—the twins would utter aloud "eternity" to make it their only thought. When Dietrich got his own room at age twelve, lying in his bed he would tap on the wall that separated the twins and the tap meant "think of God."[1]

An Atheist

Not all who talk about heaven are as serious as the young Bonhoeffer twins. When an atheist takes on heaven we might do well to listen. Julian Barnes, in his book *A History of the World in 10 1/2 Chapters,* lampoons those who think they know about heaven.[2] Barnes imagines his own kind of heaven. In this imagined place, he gets to have multiple breakfasts in bed and long, long baths. He does everything on his bucket list: cruises, exploring a jungle, some painting. He falls in love a number of times with many different women, and he meets every important footballer. But in his guesses, Barnes has noted, after a time there is a strange absence: there is no God in heaven.

So Barnes has a conversation with Margaret, his imagined guide.

"I don't want to sound ungrateful," I said cautiously, "but where's God?"
"God. Do you want God? Is that what you want?". . . .
"I didn't think it depended on me in any way."
"Of course it does."

Then Barnes provides an alarming, but brutally honest, description of so much speculation about heaven these days.

"Heaven is democratic these days," she said. Then added, "Or at least, it is if
   you want it to be."

"What do you mean, democratic?"

"We don't impose Heaven on people anymore," she said. "We listen to their
   needs. If they want it, they can have it; if not, not. And then of course they
   get the sort of Heaven they want."

"And what sort do they want on the whole?"

"Well, they want a continuation of life, that's what we find. But . . . better. . . ."

"Sex, golf, shopping, dinner, meeting famous people and not feeling bad?" I
   asked a bit defensively.[3]

We need this Mark Twain–like lampooning of what we would like heaven to be
because it forces us to take a deeper look at what we believe. Is heaven nothing but
projections of what we enjoy here and now? The British philosopher, David Hume,
once told James Boswell that "he did not wish to be immortal." Surprised, Boswell
pushed for more. Why would he not want immortality? Hume said it was because
"he was very well in this state of being, and that the chances were very much against
his being so well in another state."[4]

I suspect more people are like Barnes than Hume. People dream of heaven being
the fulfillment of our longings and wishes, the healing of our hurts, and the answer
to all our questions. We think of heaven as far more than delicious food and out-
standing sex, more possessions, reunions with friends and family, more money and
pleasure, and more glory.

AUTHORS

My friend and author Karen Spears Zacharias has a view of heaven too, and it's close
to mine. So, of course, I think (and hope) she's right:

It's hard to visualize Heaven. To be honest, streets of gold and gated communities don't interest me much. And I only want a mansion if there is a staff
like on *Downton Abbey* to take care of it.

My idea of heaven would be a home at the end of a dirt road on Mobile Bay. A place surrounded by white roses, a porch for pondering, and birds— redbirds, bluebirds, mockingbirds, and even a visit from [her own] Mama bird, every now and then.[5]

Lots of people think of heaven as a church service, or at least as Eternal Sundays. My wife, Kris, is an introvert. By Sunday at about noon she has had enough and needs a rest from all those people talking and singing and hugging and asking questions and telling stories and sometimes standing a bit too close. So Karen's heaven is Kris's kind of heaven too, though both would gladly toss in some kids and grandkids. Bring on the children and grandchildren, but at the end of a long road, quiet and peaceful. That's heavenly.

Here's how Ernest Hemingway described his idea of heaven in a 1925 letter to F. Scott Fitzgerald:

To me heaven would be a big bull ring with me holding two barrera seats and a trout stream outside that no one else was allowed to fish in and two lovely houses in the town; one where I would have my wife and children and be monogamous and love them truly and well and the other where I would have my nine beautiful mistresses on 9 different floors. . . . Then there would be a fine church like in Pamplona where I could go and be confessed on the way from one house to the other and I would get on my horse and ride out with my son to my bull ranch . . . and toss coins to all my illegitimate children that lived [along] the road.[6]

At least he's colorful in his ribald manliness and imagination.

A Movie Star

Not only do we all have theories about what heaven is like, we are not afraid to announce who will be there and who won't be let in. Most vote against Hitler, and all but the grumps vote in Mother Teresa. The movie star Jane Fonda, who has never hesitated to share her opinions publically, announced her decision on the eternal fate of her ex-husband, mega-millionaire Ted Turner. From CNN:

> Fonda said she believes Turner's childhood traumas left him so protective of himself that he had trouble opening up emotionally. But, she said, he does want to get into heaven. And, she said, he's a shoo-in.
>
> Finally, with our 23 minutes with Turner ticking down, we've gotten his full attention. We let [Ted] in on what Fonda has told CNN about his heavenly prospects:
>
> "Given his childhood," Fonda said, "he should've become a dictator. He should've become a not nice person. The miracle is that he became what he is. A man who will go to heaven, and there'll be a lot of animals up there welcoming him, animals that have been brought back from the edge of extinction because of Ted. He's turned out to be a good guy. And he says he's not religious. But he, the whole time I was with him, every speech—and he likes to give speeches—he always ends his speech with 'God bless.' And he'll get into heaven. He's a miracle."
>
> Turner listened intently. There was a long pause. Was he tearing up? Finally, he spoke. "She said that?"
>
> Another long pause. "Well, I sure don't want to go to hell." . . .
>
> [Ted] has said he "can't see myself sitting on a cloud and playing the harp day in and day out." So what is Ted Turner's notion of heaven?
>
> "Montana in the summer."[7]

Everyone seems to have a vivid imagination when it comes to heaven.

QUESTIONS ABOUT THE HEAVEN QUESTION

We ask in this surprising welter of guesses and opinions and hopes: How can we know what heaven will be like? (Read on.) Is heaven an illusion? (No, but sometimes it is.) Is it merely in our brains? (Sometimes.) Is it a grand projection of what we most want for our world? (For some, it is.) Is it a spiritual realm unlike what we experience on earth? (In part.) Can we know who goes there (or who doesn't)? (Yes.) Is there a way to know about heaven in more detail? (Read on.)[8] What about all the near-death experiences people are writing about and some are tempted to fabricate? (Keep reading.)

In what follows I want to sketch the most important ideas about heaven that come from the Bible. Then in the last section we will turn to the top ten questions about heaven. We can't answer most of the questions until we first get a solid grip on the big ideas about heaven. It is to those ideas that we now turn.

Imaginations of the Imaginative

The Bible First

> Heaven is itself the metaphor of metaphors, for a metaphor
> opens to more and more meaning, and heaven is an
> unbordered meadow of meaning. Heaven is where language
> collapses into perfect language and then further—into the
> truth beyond language. Heaven is what things really mean.
>
> — Jeffrey Burton Russell

Have you ever wondered where we get our ideas about heaven? For instance, where did anyone get the idea that in heaven we'd be playing harps or singing all the time, or that we'd be in an eternal church service? Or that we will fly like the angels? Take a minute to think about your most precious ideas about heaven, and then ask where you got these ideas. I'll tell you my favorite idea: that heaven will be like a posh golf course as the evening sun begins to dip behind the trees and the grasses begin to cool and collect dew. Then I have to acknowledge that I have this view of heaven because I love the experience of being on a golf course in the evening.

So where do we get our ideas about heaven?

- From mom and dad? Yes.
- From trusted pastors and teachers? Yes.
- From Internet blogs? Yes.
- From our own experience or the experiences of others? Yes.
- From our hopes, wishes, and expectations? Yes.
- From the greats of literature—Dante, Milton, Bunyan? Yes, yes, yes.
- From movies? Yes.
- From the Bible? I'm not so sure.

It might surprise you to know that the classic creeds of the Christian faith—the attempts by the best thinkers in the church to get back to the basics of the faith—have very little to say about heaven (or hell). Take the granddaddy of all the creeds, the Apostles' Creed, where we learn that Jesus descended into hell and ascended into heaven, where he now rules, and that he'll come again to judge the living and the dead. The last two words in the creed affirm that we believe in "life everlasting." You are forgiven if you can't help but mutter, *"C'mon, you gotta give us more than that!"*

The most complete of all the creeds, the Nicene Creed, provides little more: "and I look for the resurrection of the dead, and the life of the world to come." Now we have "the life of the world to come" to expand on "life everlasting."[1]

Skip ahead centuries to the most influential Presbyterian confession, the Westminster Confession of Faith, which tells us, "For then shall the righteous go into everlasting life, and receive that fullness of joy and refreshing, which shall come from the presence of the Lord."[2] If you were hoping that the reformers would go deeper in clarifying our understanding of heaven, you now have "fullness of joy and refreshing" to add to the sketchy descriptions contained in the previous confessions.

We still don't know much about what heaven will be like. One response to this lack of clarity is to milk the texts we do have for all they're worth. Sometimes this helps illumine. On other occasions, where the text is stretched too far, it obscures.

All of this taken together—our insatiable curiosity about heaven and the scant detail provided in the leading creeds and confessions—points to a huge problem we all face.

Two Views of Heaven, Each Easily Exaggerated

We want heaven to be what we believe heaven *ought* to be. Said differently, people imagine that heaven will be very similar to what they think it will be. We see this in Diane Keaton's documentary film *Heaven: The Ultimate Coming Attraction*. One imaginative view of heaven after another fills the screen.

The same imagination drives images of heaven in other familiar movies. *It's a Wonderful Life, For Heaven's Sake, Monty Python's The Meaning of Life, Made in Heaven,* and even *Highway to Heaven.* And we haven't even gotten to country music, where hopes for heaven are listed in Marty Robbins's classic "Hillbilly Heaven." In other genres, we have Eric Clapton's haunting "Tears in Heaven" and oft-sung hymns such as "In the Sweet By and By" and "Beulah Land."

Then there are books of enormous influence such as *The Divine Comedy, Paradise Lost,* and *Pilgrim's Progress,* and even the chronicle of near-death experiences in Raymond Moody's *Life After Life.* Each author, in a variety of ways, has imagined heaven and shaped the beliefs of Christians. Now toss some art into the mix, including Michelangelo's famous *Final Judgment* that depicts heaven and hell looming over the heads of those who are judged. So many images of heaven crowd our thinking that we'll be lucky if we are able to get beyond them in order to consider what the Bible actually says.

It is helpful to remember that the overactive imaginations of the imaginative are often nothing more than . . . fanciful imaginings!

Because we have such wonderfully fertile and, yes, God-given imaginations, we can plot a history of how the church has thought about heaven.[3] That story can be captured in two sophisticated words: a *theocentric* heaven (God centered) and a *kingdom-centric* heaven (world-transformed centered).

In the theocentric heaven, the focus and unending characteristic is praise of God. The kingdom-centric heaven focuses on the new heavens and the new earth, where God's people will live with one another after the pattern of life God intended for them.

Here's a chart of these two views:

Theocentric	Kingdom-Centric
God	God and God's people
Glory of God	God's perfect society
Mode of life: worship	Worship and fellowship
Atmosphere: holiness	Justice and peace
Gathered for worship	Social engagement
Family eliminated	Family perfected
Fellowship diminished	Fellowship emphasized
Location: heaven up there	New heavens, new earth
Spiritual existence	Embodied existence

In the history of the church, pastors, priests, and parents have cooked the books by taking sides and exaggerating one of these views at the expense of the other. As a result, we deserve some scorn from Mark Twain. More than a few times I have read Twain's splendid revelation of how ordinary boys (Tom Sawyer and Huck Finn) respond to the theocentric heaven ledger that becomes an eternal Sunday-morning service of sing and sermon and sing some more. Here is Huck's take on heaven:

> Now she [Miss Watson, "a tolerable slim old maid"] had got a start, and she went on and told me all about the good place [heaven]. She said all a body would have to do there was to go around all day long with a harp and sing forever and ever. So I didn't think much of it. But I never said so. I asked her if she reckoned Tom Sawyer would go there, and she said not by a consider-able sight. I was glad about that, because I wanted him and me to be together.[4]

A similar problem surfaces when you listen to the kingdom-centric side. Some of these descriptions of heaven are so ordinary, they make me wonder if heaven might be a grand but endless celebration with news networks covering developments as they occur. A very thoughtful writer, Arthur Roberts, asks the right question about too much emphasis on the social aspect of heaven: "Who wants a parade and a barbecue every day?"[5] I would add, "Who wants to be at a church camp living in bunks and eating in an open cafeteria forever?"

What we need is balance between the God-centered heaven and kingdom-centered heaven. To get that balance we need to return to the Bible. The Bible shapes our imaginations with bundles of images and metaphors and visions about heaven. God made us to love God and to love others. Heaven will be our living both of these callings perfectly.

TWO KINDS OF PEOPLE IN HEAVEN

Two people come to mind who represent each side of a heaven marked by loving God *and* loving others. When reflecting on the theocentric side, I think of A. W. Tozer and one of his memorable lines: "I can safely say, on the authority of all that is revealed in the Word of God, that any man or woman on this earth who is bored and turned off by worship is not ready for heaven."[6] Tozer, whose life was controlled by his desire to commune with God in prayer and worship, believed heaven would be a world of worship.

The second person is Martin Luther, who (for our purposes) represents the kingdom-centric view. One of the least known stories about Luther—except to Lutherans—is how he "acquired" a wife. Remember Luther was an Augustinian Roman Catholic celibate when his readings of Paul's letters drove home that he was made right with God, not by his multitude of acts of discipline—like fasting and beating his back with a whip—but by God's grace. He launched nothing less than a revolution, and one of the implications of that revolution was that converted Catholic priests could marry. How did Luther get his wife? Glad you asked:

> In the nearby town of Torgau was a respected senior citizen named Leonard Kopp. A member of the town council and former Torgau tax collector, he had the contract to deliver barrels of smoked herring to the cloister in Nimbschen which housed the twelve unhappy nuns. Exactly how Kopp did it is unknown, but somehow when he arrived, his canvas-covered wagon seemed to be carrying twelve barrels of smoked herring, and when he left it seemed to be loaded with twelve empty barrels underneath the canvas. But the barrels were not empty.

Two days later, nine nuns (three had returned to their parents' homes) were delivered to Martin Luther's doorstep, and it was Luther's job to find either positions or husbands for them.[7]

As one historian described it, those nuns had been trained to do little more than sing and pray and get ready for a theocentric heaven! Luther eventually found a place for each of the nuns except one, Katie von Bora. A friend of Luther's wanted to marry her, but the suitor's parents denied their son's wish. After a few attempts by others, including Luther, to find a match for Katie, she announced she'd only marry if she could marry the likes of Luther himself. He asked his parents' permission for this barrel-delivered nun-turned-Protestant, they said, "Yes," and Luther married Katie. Their wonderful story of love and marriage will be told in heaven over and over. And I'm sure if Luther and Katie have anything to do with it, they'll tell the story over beers. After all, Luther often called Katie his "brewer."[8]

In heaven, Tozer and Luther will sit down together. Tozer, if my reading of him is correct, will have to loosen up, while Luther might have to clean up his act a bit. Heaven will be a glorious union of delight in God and delight in one another, of worship and fellowship.

But there is so much more to learn about heaven, and I don't think we need to appeal to overdeveloped imaginations to learn what it will be like. So I ask a simple question: What happens if we subject our view of heaven to the Bible? When we think and pray and talk about heaven, it is important to begin with the right ideas. And the single most important idea—that heaven is God's promise to the world—is often ignored. The Bible's promise is the place to begin all talk about heaven.

Part Two

THE HEAVEN PROMISE

The single-most important fact the Bible teaches about heaven is this:

God has promised Heaven.

If Heaven is God's promise, then Heaven is as good as God is faithful.

Before we can answer questions like these: How do I get there? Who will be there? What will heaven be like? we need to pause to consider the Bible's teaching that Heaven is God's promise to the world.

We also need to see that the heart of the Heaven Promise is the resurrection of Jesus, whose resurrected body becomes the template of our resurrection bodies.

We will also discover that there are two senses to what *Heaven* means in the Bible:

1. A present heaven (lowercase)
2. A final kingdom of God, a future Heaven (uppercase)

Later in Part Two, I will make a case for these two senses of heaven and spell the first one "heaven" and the second one "Heaven." One of the most comforting truths about Heaven is that Jesus's resurrection encourages us to face death standing in the empty tomb.

Heaven, It's a Promise!

God Promises Us Heaven

A good God would not create us with the kind of aspirations
we have and then leave those aspirations unsatisfied.

— Jerry Walls

One word outshines all others in helping us grab hold of heaven. It is the word *promise*. Heaven is God's promise that he will accomplish what he has said he will accomplish. Heaven is as secure as God's promise, as good as God's faithfulness, and as gracious as God's love. Heaven: it's God's promise to us.

The promise began when God elbowed Abram in the ribs at the ripe young age of seventy-five, in a place not far east and north of today's Aleppo in Syria,* and told him to get all his stuff together and go to a special place. So Abram gathered up his wife, at that time still named Sarai, his nephew Lot and his family, their slaves, and cartloads of possessions, and walked or trotted south through Damascus and down into the Jordan Rift Valley. They continued over the river into the arid hills north of Jerusalem. Before the trip, God promised Abram that he and Sarai would have

---

* Abram was dwelling in a placed called Harran. The account is based on Genesis 12; 15.

children and their children would produce children who would produce children until his descendants would become a "great nation." He also promised Abram that he would have a "great name" and that he would be "blessed." The blessing came in the mysterious and baffling promise that "all peoples on earth will be blessed through you." God promised this to Abram:

1. Nation-sized family
2. Global reputation
3. Abundance and flourishing
4. Influence on the whole world

During the trip, Abram must have pondered that set of global promises, and I would suspect he was excited about the future. God, for some reason, grabbed an obscure man living in the deserts of the Middle East and *promised* him he would have *cosmic significance.*

It's one thing to promise something, it's another to bring it to pass, and it is yet another to trust the promiser. Abram and Sarai had been trying to make babies for years, but with no luck. Yet that was part of the blessing and it had been promised. So an impatient Abram complained to God: "You have given me no children." Getting a little passive aggressive, Abram then informed God of his plan: "A servant in my household will be my heir."

The God of patience responded with this exchange in Genesis 15:

God: "This man [Abram's servant] will not be your heir, but a son who is your own flesh and blood will be your heir."

Abram must have been heard muttering, "Tell me something new."

God took Abram outside and said, "Look up at the sky and count the stars—if indeed you can count them." Then he said to him, "So shall your offspring be."

Abram then took a giant step forward because he trusted the great God of great promises:

Abram believed the Lord, and he credited it to him as righteousness.

Abraham and Sarah, after their change of names,* got far more than they could have imagined. There are almost six million Jews—Abraham's descendants—living in the State of Israel today. Just under six million Jews live in the United States, and some two million descendants of Abraham are scattered in other parts of the world. It all began when God promised to Abram that someday God would make him—this solitary man with a solitary wife—a great nation.

The entire Bible—from Genesis to Revelation—is based on this one promise. The God of the Bible is a God who makes promises. This God can be relied upon to make good on those promises. Heaven is the promise made to Abraham in its eternal form.† When we understand Heaven as God's promise, it is transformative.

TAPS OR REVEILLE?

For instance, it can transform a funeral. At death, do we play only mournful, day-ending, time-is-over taps or do we carry on to play reveille as well? If we can see our way through death to the Heaven Promise, the music of a funeral can be transformed. Evangelist Billy Graham once told a story about a significant funeral, that of Great Britain's wartime Prime Minister, Winston Churchill:

> Years ago, Winston Churchill planned his own funeral. And he did so with the hope of the resurrection and eternal life, which he firmly believed in. And he instructed after the benediction that a bugler positioned high in the dome of St. Paul's Cathedral would play Taps, the universal signal that says the day is over.[1]

Taps sounds the notes of death and those notes can be sobering and melancholic.

---

* Abram changes to Abraham, from "exalted father" to "father of many." Sarai changes to Sarah, though the meaning seems to have been the same: "princess." This is found in Genesis 17.

† Hebrews 11:13–16 makes this clear: "All these people were still living by faith when they died. They did not receive the things promised; they only saw them and welcomed them from a distance, admitting that they were foreigners and strangers on earth. People who say such things show that they are looking for a country of their own. If they had been thinking of the country they had left, they would have had opportunity to return. Instead, they were longing for a better country—a heavenly one. Therefore God is not ashamed to be called their God, for he has prepared a city for them."

But Churchill planned that the last notes to be sounded would not be the taps. Billy Graham continued:

> But then came a very dramatic moment as Churchill had instructed. Another bugler was placed on the other side of the massive dome, and he played the notes of Reveille, the universal signal that a new day has dawned and it is time to arise. That was Churchill's testimony that at the end of history, the last note will not be Taps, it'll be Reveille.[2]

The reveille swallows up the sounds of taps and declares for all to hear that God has promised heaven, that the taps signaling the death of the day will not be the last sound. Heaven is that kind of promise.

PROMISES, PROMISES, PROMISES

Herbert Lockyer in his famous collection called *All the Promises of the Bible* counts more than eight thousand promises in the Bible![3] The Bible I just opened has 1,352 pages, and that comes to 5.9 promises per page! The Bible could be retitled *God's Multitude of Promises* or *The Book of Promises*.

What is involved in making a promise? Let's go back to Abram and the big promise. There are five elements to a promise:

- The promis*er* who makes the promise: **God**
- The promis*ee* to whom the promise is made: **Abram (and Sarai)**
- The *substance* of the promise: **great nation, blessing**
- The *covenantal* form making the promise legally binding: **God walking between the animals***
- The *acceptance:* **Abram** chooses to accept the promise

Why this discussion about how promises work? Very simple: *Heaven is God's eternal promise.* Heaven can't be proven by logic; it can't be discovered by scientists;

---

* God entered between the pieces of animals to say to Abram, "You can do this to me if I am not true to my promise." That is, "Slay me—the God of the universe—if I don't make good on my promise to you, Abram!"

it can't be established by near-death experiences. Heaven is as good as God, the Promiser. Heaven is a promise, and the promisees (you and I) participate in the promise by trusting the One who makes the promise.

THE HEAVEN PROMISE

In the previous chapter we looked at the history of heaven—or at least, the history of leading views on heaven—but there is a more important history. And that is the history of the Heaven Promise in the Bible. We can't go into the entire history here, but I want to provide a sampling of the Bible's Heaven promises. Please take the time to read them slowly and let them impact you for what they are: the Heaven Promise.* Imagine these words being read in a theater with a round of applause after each line. And by the time we get to the end, we are celebrating in a standing ovation to God for the glory of the Heaven Promise.

From Jesus

Do not be afraid, little flock, for your Father has been pleased to give you the kingdom.

I am the resurrection and the life. The one who believes in me will live, even though they die.

Do not let your hearts be troubled. You believe in God; believe also in me. My Father's house has many rooms; if that were not so, would I have told you that I am going there to prepare a place for you? And if I go and prepare a place for you, I will come back and take you to be with me that you also may be where I am.

Truly I tell you, today you will be with me in paradise.

Jesus promises heaven, his resurrection paves the way, and it begins the day we die.

---

* Luke 12:32; John 11:25; 14:1–3; Luke 23:43; 1 Thessalonians 4:16; 1 Corinthians 6:14; 15:54; 2 Corinthians 4:14; 5:1, 8; Ephesians 1:18; 1 Timothy 4:8; Hebrews 12:28; 1 Peter 1:3–4; Revelation 22:3–4.

From Paul

For the Lord himself will come down from heaven, with a loud command, with the voice of the archangel and with the trumpet call of God, and the dead in Christ will rise first.

By his power God raised the Lord from the dead, and he will raise us also.

When the perishable has been clothed with the imperishable, and the mortal with immortality, then the saying that is written will come true: "Death has been swallowed up in victory."

. . . because we know that the one who raised the Lord Jesus from the dead will also raise us with Jesus and present us with you to himself.

For we know that if the earthly tent we live in is destroyed, we have a building from God, an eternal house in heaven, not built by human hands.

We are confident, I say, and would prefer to be away from the body and at home with the Lord.

I pray that the eyes of your heart may be enlightened in order that you may know the hope to which he has called you, the riches of his glorious inheritance in his holy people.

For physical training is of some value, but godliness has value for all things, holding promise for both the present life and the life to come.

Paul promises heaven; the resurrection of Jesus makes it possible, and when it happens death will die its own eternal death. Good riddance! True to Jesus, Paul says the Heaven Promise is fully revealed the moment we die.

Therefore, since we are receiving a kingdom that cannot be shaken, let us be thankful, and so worship God acceptably with reverence and awe.

Praise be to the God and Father of our Lord Jesus Christ! In his great mercy he has given us new birth into a living hope through the resurrection of Jesus Christ from the dead, and into an inheritance that can never perish, spoil or fade. This inheritance is kept in heaven for you.

No longer will there be any curse. The throne of God and of the Lamb will be in the city, and his servants will serve him. They will see his face, and his name will be on their foreheads.

What we do now prepares us for that promise, and the promise is guaranteed for eternity. It means God will be right here with us.

Each of these fifteen promises is as good as God's first promise made to Abram. As the history of the Heaven Promise unfolds, we begin to see that the Abram promise becomes the Heaven Promise. But I have saved the best promise for last: *the Heaven Promise as the new heavens and the new earth.*

At the end of the Heaven Promise is an expression that tells the whole story: "new heavens and new earth." God first promised this through Isaiah, and later through Peter and then through John:*

See, I will create
　　new heavens and a new earth.
The former things will not be remembered,
　　nor will they come to mind.

No longer will they build houses and others live in them,
　　or plant and others eat.
For as the days of a tree,
　　so will be the days of my people;
my chosen ones will long enjoy
　　the work of their hands.

But in keeping with his promise we are looking forward to *a new heaven and a new earth,* where righteousness dwells.

Then I saw *"a new heaven and a new earth,"* for the first heaven and the first earth had passed away, and there was no longer any sea.

---

* Isaiah 65:17, 22; 2 Peter 3:13; Revelation 21:1

And even then the apostle Paul would say to us, "That's nothing. Listen to this one from Isaiah that you did not quote":

No one has heard,
　no ear has perceived,
no eye has seen any God besides you,
　who acts on behalf of those who wait for him.*

No matter how grand or how incomprehensible heaven will be, heaven is nothing if it is not God's promise. Here is one more heavenly promise from the Bible, this one from the apostle Paul. In Romans 8, Paul reveals there are circles of groaning—the Spirit, the children of God, and all of creation. What is creation groaning about? For its own redemption in the new heavens and the new earth!

For the creation was subjected to frustration, not by its own choice, but by the will of the one who subjected it, in hope that the *creation itself will be liberated* from its bondage to decay and brought into the freedom and glory of the children of God.†

Heaven is God's promise to you and to me. The God who promises is the promise God.

The Reliability of the Heaven Promise

Remember, the reliability of the promise is ensured by five elements.
　God is making the promise,
　God's promise is *heaven,*
　God makes this promise to *us* and for *us,*
　God has *entered into a covenant* with us to make the

---

* Isaiah 64:4
† Romans 8:20–21

Heaven Promise good, a binding covenant on which God
stakes his life and integrity,
and we are asked to *trust God's promise.*

If God has been faithful to Abraham, and he has, then surely God will be faithful to Jesus and to the apostles. Heaven is God's promise to all of us, but we must accept the promise and trust God.

When God walked between Abram's animals, God was making it visibly clear that his promise could be trusted. But that ancient event is overwhelmed in importance by one dramatic, death-ending act God performed long after Abram was no longer on the earth. Some two thousand years later we received the gift of the first Easter, when the tomb's cover was removed by the power of God. The heart of the Heaven Promise is Easter.

4

The Heart of the Promise

Jesus Was Raised

> Christmas itself has now far outstripped Easter in
> popular culture as the real celebratory center of the
> Christian year—a move that completely reverses the
> New Testament's emphasis.
>
> —N. T. Wright

Believers in the God who promises heaven can hear reveille in a world filled with taps. But that doesn't mean we don't hear taps. Those to whom God promises heaven have loved ones who die, and they experience the grief of death's stunning, silent separation. The pain can be almost unbearable, the grief numbing us. Tears flow and the dark night of our loved one's absence may haunt our every moment. We wonder if we can get through it. The Heaven Promise may excite us, but the reality of death can suck the joy from life.

Some, seeking distraction from the pain, turn to humor and quote W. C. Fields's famous character Sam Bisbee, who said, "It's a funny ol' world . . . Man's lucky if he gets out of it alive."[1] Or that great English writer Somerset Maugham might give us a few moments of respite: "Dying is a very dull, dreary affair. . . . And my advice to you is to have nothing whatever to do with it."[2] And Woody Allen once said, "It's not that I am afraid to die. I just don't want to be there when it happens."[3]

That's funny and ironic, but let's admit the deeper truth: all the quips inspired by death—and the avoidance of it—bring no comfort when the one you love most dies. At that moment, you don't need humor.

Where are you to go?

THE GRIEF OF C. S. LEWIS

Let's start with a story about C. S. Lewis and his wife, Joy Davidman, who died a premature and painful death. Lewis, whose fiction and Christian thinking have captured more than one generation, opened his pained heart to the world in *A Grief Observed*. In fact, in some ways he has paved the way for others because many have found his expressions of grief can help them tell their own story of grief. Perhaps most importantly, we learn from Lewis the importance of admitting our grief and what it does to our perception of the world and ourselves:

> Not only writing but even reading a letter is too much. Even shaving. What does it matter now whether my cheek is rough or smooth?[4]

Lewis believed in God and in the resurrection and he never let up in that faith. But in candor many have learned to appreciate, he admitted his faith did not seem to offer much help. Lewis had entered into a dark, cold, penetrating fog. He told us—and we read his words feeling a shiver up the spine—what he found when he went to God in the throes of his grief:

> But go to Him when your need is desperate, when all other help is vain, and what do you find? A door slammed in your face, and a sound of bolting and double bolting on the inside.[5]

Not only did grief seem to consume his days but he began to grieve about his own grieving. Many have learned from him that grief can be like storm clouds emptying cold rain in a foggy storm. We want it to get over but it lingers on and on and on. Looking into that cold night, Lewis echoed another common experience with grief: He couldn't find Joy; he couldn't touch Joy; he couldn't hear Joy's voice because she was dead. He asked, "Is that word so difficult to learn?" He had come face-to-face with the personal reality of his wife's death.

When people offered him simplistic but wet blanket words they thought would be comforting, he rejected them because he was facing Joy's absence and a world in which he would live without her.

And then, some of the most uncomforting words ever from the pen of a man whose words have comforted us all: "Talk to me about the truth of religion and I'll listen gladly. Talk to me about the duty of religion and I'll listen submissively. But don't come talking to me about the consolations of religion or I shall suspect you don't understand." His grief wouldn't let up, and his faith offered him no consolation. Grief is real, and we ask again, What are we to do? Where can we go?

But somewhere on Lewis's journey the fog began to lift. He began to sense that doors to life were beginning to open, that the pain was there and he would hobble the rest of life because of the grief he had experienced. In fact, as he put it, "I am learning to get about on crutches. . . . But I shall never be a biped again."[6]

These words remind me of what Malcolm Muggeridge, that courageous British journalist who trusted in Christ late in life, said about his mother after her husband, Malcolm's father, died:

> When my father died my mother closed his eyes, with a certain irritation at
> their refusing to open again, but never accustomed herself to life without
> him. The bed in which they had slept side by side through so many nights
> had two hollows in it; with the other unoccupied, my mother lay disconso-
> lately in hers.[7]

Whether your grief is a hollowed bed, an empty chair, an unopened book, an untended flower bed, the unused bicycle, or that special restaurant to which you can no longer go, death leaves one hollow after another. And the ones who live on often limp for a season.

The big questions that grief drives us to ask are: Will the pain end? Will the tears dry up? Will we find joy in life once again?

And again, we ask, "What can we do? Where are we to go?"

IN THE FOG WE HEAR THE HEART OF THE PROMISE

Some say we can do nothing and there's nowhere to turn, and they might even suggest we will just have to abide in a depressed fog with the little hope we can muster. After all, in the inimitable words of N. T. Wright, "All language about the future, as any economist or politician will tell you, is simply a set of signposts pointing into a fog." But will the fog lift? Can we find our way through the fog?

Listen to the words of Wright because he declares that the fog will not have the last word. He answers our questions with a question: "And—supposing someone came forward out of the fog to meet us?"[8] That "someone" is Jesus, who burns off the mists of fog in the blazing heat of his resurrection. Brilliant. Grief and the fog, but in the fog we discover the One who can make the sun visible again.

Everything about heaven—and I mean absolutely nothing gets left out—is based on Jesus's resurrection. Our heaven hope begins with a baby conceived prior to the marriage bed through a miracle, with a mother who was rejected by her contemporaries and a father who no doubt raised the eyebrows of many observant Jews when he married the pregnant Mary.

It begins with a young Jewish man standing on a hill teaching the Law in ways that penetrated hearts just as it challenged current conventions. It begins with a rabbi-like man who performed astounding miracles that anticipated God's power to make life anew. The same man who gathered disciples from every trade and corner of life, who accepted in scandalous ways women who had unsavory reputations, who had the moxie to challenge both Jewish and Roman leaders in ways that made the peasants tell jokes in private. It began with a man who entered Jerusalem already doomed and who was tried in ways that embarrass even the most unscrupulous of lawyers. This man was crucified—bloody and exposed and shamed in public. And he died.

But just as he predicted, he was rumored to be alive three days later. And just as he declared, he was raised by God from the dead. That's where it all begins. With Jesus—his birth, life, mission, death, and resurrection.

The Heaven Promise is as good as the resurrection of Jesus, and if Jesus was raised from the dead, the fog of death and grief can give way to the sunshine of God's new heavens and new earth.

HE IS RISEN!

The Christian's heaven hope is founded completely on the resurrection of Jesus. No resurrection of Jesus, no Christian heaven. This is why Lisa Miller, after studying heaven, confessed her unbelief in heaven because of her unbelief in resurrection: "For me—personally speaking—resurrection is the biggest obstacle to belief in heaven. As much as I'd like to imagine that in heaven I'll get my pre-baby body back—its pleasures, its stamina—I just don't. We get old, we wear out, we die. Time never moves backward."[9] She gets an award for rugged honesty.

But should we not say that the time she thinks never moves backward actually moves at brilliant speed into a future? Yes, that's the way to put it. The resurrection doesn't turn the clock backward; instead, it propels the present into the final kingdom of God.

Can we reasonably believe that Jesus was raised from the dead? Yes, and for four convincing reasons:

First, the tomb was empty. No one produced a body and said, "Here he is! Now knock it off with this resurrection nonsense!" An empty tomb leaves us with only two reasonable options: either someone removed the body—which means that the women and disciples lied or were mistaken—or God raised Jesus. Mark's gospel gives us this description:

When the Sabbath was over, Mary Magdalene, Mary the mother of James, and Salome bought spices so that they might go to anoint Jesus' body. Very early on the first day of the week, just after sunrise, they were on their way to the tomb and they asked each other, "Who will roll the stone away from the entrance of the tomb?"

But when they looked up, they saw that the stone, which was very large, had been rolled away. As they entered the tomb, they saw a young man dressed in a white robe sitting on the right side, and they were alarmed.

"Don't be alarmed," he said. "You are looking for Jesus the Nazarene, who was crucified. He has risen! He is not here. See the place where they laid him.*

Second, some people claimed that they encountered Jesus after his death. Here is the barest account of these appearances:

He was raised on the third day according to the Scriptures, and . . . he *appeared* to Cephas, and then to the Twelve. After that, he *appeared* to more than five hundred of the brothers and sisters at the same time, most of whom are still living, though some have fallen asleep. Then he *appeared* to James, then to all the apostles, and last of all he *appeared* to me also, as to one abnormally born.†

Some people report having had an encounter with a dead loved one. But no one who has reported such an encounter then goes to the grave to discover the body missing. The Christian claim is that the tomb was empty *and* he appeared to a large number of witnesses.

Third, there is no evidence that the post-resurrection witnesses had any opportunity to fabricate false testimony. You can test this yourself by trying to figure out from the Gospels what happened to whom, when, and in what order. Sit down with all four Gospels, turn to the Resurrection narratives, and then sort out the order of the events.‡

The New Testament does not record an ordered narrative with a sequential story arc. Instead, it is a scrapbook of undated stories that, taken together, give a full picture of the Resurrection. The story is told, but it is impossible to put the events in sequence with any confidence.

---

* Mark 16:1–6
† 1 Corinthians 15:4–8
‡ Matthew 28; Mark 16; Luke 24; John 20–21

This strongly suggests that those who testified to Jesus's resurrection did not confer with each other to get their stories straight. If the Resurrection claim is fabrication and the disciples and women had colluded to cover up the truth, then the stories about the empty tomb and the appearances of Jesus would work together to present a coherent story. I join the many historians who have impartially studied the Gospels to say *the absence of collusion among the storytellers establishes credibility for the Gospel claims of the resurrection of Jesus.*

*The fourth and final argument: the first persons to witness the empty tomb were women.** Historians remind us that Jewish courts in the first century rarely would permit a woman to testify. But believers did not alter their story to make it more convincing in light of contemporary practices. Rather, they told the story as it happened. Women were the first people to see the tomb empty and the first to see the resurrected Jesus. If Jesus's followers had been fabricating the resurrection of Jesus, they would never have included a woman, especially not Mary Magdalene, in their cast of witnesses.

In conclusion, consider what this generation's most significant thinker on the resurrection of Jesus, N. T. Wright, has to say:

> Far and away the best historical explanation is that Jesus of Nazareth, having been thoroughly dead and buried, really was raised to life on the third day with a renewed body.[10]

THE WORLD'S BIGGEST *IF*

This leads to history's biggest IF clause: If Jesus was raised from the dead, then what? The apostle Paul laid down three concessions if Jesus was *not* raised. We can turn his negatives around and run them in the other direction: If Christ was raised from the dead, (1) we are witnesses of the truth, (2) our preaching is true and our faith is sound, and (3) our sin is unraveled and erased and we can be made right with God—for eternity.†

---

* Mark 16:1–8, John 20:11–17
† 1 Corinthians 15:12–19

If he was raised from the dead, the Heaven Promise is secure.

That is the biggest *if* in history.

Once again, *everything* about heaven is based on Jesus's resurrection. If Jesus was raised from the dead, and we are confident he was, what we believe about heaven is transformed. This must be said another way: what many believe about heaven has little (or nothing) to do with Jesus's resurrection, and as a result they have overactive imaginations that color their thinking about heaven. What C. S. Lewis will experience in heaven with Joy Davidman takes on a whole new look if we use Jesus's resurrection as a model for what heaven will be like.

We can now ask a wonderful new question and anticipate whether the answer will transform what we think about heaven:

> What is heaven like . . .
> if we take the resurrection of Jesus seriously?

The Christian Belief

We Will Have Bodies Like the Body of Jesus

I am somewhere unbelievably wonderful right now.

— Stefanie Spielman

C hris Spielman was one of the most competitive athletes ever to have played football at Ohio State University, and after that for three NFL teams. When his wife was diagnosed with breast cancer, Chris found himself at a crossroads. His football story ended, and his beautiful love story with Stefanie was reshaped by the resurrection of Jesus.[1]

In 1998, having suffered a serious neck and spine injury himself, Chris took a year off to attend to Stefanie's battle with cancer. In a few years she was diagnosed with Stage IV metastatic breast cancer. A recent book has called cancer "the emperor of all maladies."[2] The Spielmans would agree, but they know the Emperor who rules over the emperor of all maladies.

Constantly strengthened by her quiet but resolute faith, Stefanie waged a twelve-year war. She battled back and forth between victories and defeats, between faith and fear, between the hope for life and the fog of death. Some days the emperor of all maladies ruled, and other days the emperor was in hiding. She and Chris raised funds for cancer research and served as a support for those who were suffering. Amazingly, Stefanie gave birth to two more children, in addition to the two she and Chris already had.

But the cancer progressed into her lungs and then into her spine and spinal fluid. Eventually death's dark forces began to be seen as cancer entered into her brain. Chris and Stefanie had been discreet but honest with their two oldest children, but the younger ones now needed to know about their mother's worsening condition.

Chris's personality was formed by a relentless work ethic from his football days. But how does a father tell a seven- and an eight-year-old about the inevitable death of their mother? When Chris got the four kids together (Maddie, Noah, Macy, and Audrey), emotion and theology found glorious expression.

> I put an arm around each one of them and said, "Mace, Aud, Mommy isn't going to get any better."
>
> They started crying. They weren't inconsolable, but the news profoundly affected them. I think, in their hearts, they knew this was coming.
>
> Then I said, "But there is one way she can get better. When she gets to heaven, she's going to get a whole new body. She's going to get to do the things that she loves to do. You know, Mom loves to run. She loves to dance. She loves to play. She'll get to do those things she loves to do, and she won't ever have to worry about being sick again. That's something we should be very, very happy about."
>
> Audrey asked, "Is her hair going to grow back?"[3]

I love Audrey's question about whether her mom's hair would grow back. If you were answering her question, it would depend on what you think heaven will be like, and that depends on what you think of Jesus's resurrection. Chris told Audrey "Yeah," then added, "it's going to be more beautiful than you ever remember it!" I would have said the same. Why? Because of what the Bible says about the resurrection of Jesus.

But let's not pretend belief in the resurrection or heaven makes all things good. Grief will stretch its chilly arms around that family as long as they live on earth.

Chris Spielman spoke about those chilly arms: "I don't think anyone can understand the connection a loved one has to every single thing a family does until that
person dies. That's when you find out how extensively they're woven into the fabric"
of all of life. Stefanie is still found "in every memory, every tradition, and every
habit."[4] Of course we should not act as if our belief in the resurrection and heaven
eliminate grief, because they don't. But heaven can electrify our hopes of reunion,
and that is why it is so important to take the resurrection of Jesus seriously when it
comes to understanding heaven.

FUZZY BELIEFS

A friend of mine said he believes in the resurrection because after one of his friends
died, she appeared to him and spoke with him. I asked if he touched her and he told
me, "No, but I could see right through her!" For some people, postmortem appearances prove the resurrection. But this fuzzy idea is not at all what the New Testament
means by *resurrection*.

Others believe that we each have a soul and that our soul is immortal, like God.
That is, we are made up of two (or three) parts: body and soul (and spirit). Such
persons believe the body may die and disintegrate into dust, but the soul lives on.
Many people think the Bible teaches this, but this is not what the Bible teaches.
Rather, it says *the body* (not just souls) will be raised. What the prophets believed
about the resurrection can be read in the incredibly fun vision of Ezekiel in the valley
with dem bones that got to rattlin' and shakin'. When God reclothed the bones with
skin and sent the spirit of life back into them, they began to walk and dance and
run.* This set of images in Ezekiel grew into the Jewish belief in the resurrection of
the body at the end of history.[5] Life after death and immortality of the soul are not
the same as resurrection of the body.

Here then is a very important point that guides and affects our view of heaven.
To believe in the *resurrection* is to believe *that we will be re-embodied for the new
heavens and the new earth.* That is, we will have transformed bodies, but we will

---

* Ezekiel 37

have bodies. Jesus ate and he drank and his disciples touched his body. N. T. Wright says it perfectly: belief in the resurrection is belief in "life *after* 'life after death.'"[6] We affirm life after death, but what we affirm even more is that it will be *an embodied life* after life after death. Heaven is designed for those kinds of bodies.

THE CHRISTIAN BELIEF

Christians don't just believe in life after death, and they don't believe merely in the immortality *of the soul.* Instead, they believe in a new embodied existence after death.

This chart illustrates the Christian belief:

Everyone believes in:	Some believe in:	Christian belief:
Death	Afterlife	A new Kingdom body
or		
Death	Life-after-death	Life after life-after-death

When we join the apostles to proclaim that Jesus was raised from the dead (which our church does every Sunday), we are claiming not just that he lives eternally or that his soul went to God. No, we are announcing that Jesus took on flesh and blood in a new body that was made for the future kingdom of God. Jesus's resurrection body transforms what we need to believe about heaven.

JESUS'S BODY IS THE FIRST BODY MADE FOR HEAVEN

In Jesus's resurrection we are face to face with the first body made for heaven. Jesus's resurrection body shows us what our bodies will be like, and therefore what heaven will be like. Maybe I need to emphasize this point: what we see in the body of the raised Jesus is what all resurrection bodies will be like.

So we ask, "What was his body like?" Here are a few of the facts from the New Testament:

First, a body in heaven will be an *ordinary, physical body, not some kind* *of luminescent glowing light.* When the disciples met Jesus on the path to Emmaus, they did not observe anything weird about his body. He seemed ordinary.[*]

Second, it will be *a body that needs food.* Yes, that's what Jesus's heavenly body "did" after his resurrection, so that is what our bodies will need to do.[†]

Third, it will be *a body with marks from our life now.* One of my favorite verses about the resurrection body of Jesus is found in Luke's gospel: "Look," Jesus said to those who wondered if it really was Jesus, "at my hands and my feet."[‡] Why there? Because the wounds from the crucifixion were visible.

Fourth, our bodies will *have powers we would classify today as supernatural. Further, our bodies may at times glow with the glory of God.* Jesus, we are told, suddenly appeared in rooms without opening doors.[§]

Facts such as these led the apostle Paul to talk about *our* resurrection bodies in these terms:

> So will it be with the resurrection of the dead. The body that is sown is
> perishable, it is raised imperishable; it is sown in dishonor, it is raised in glory;
> it is sown in weakness, it is raised in power; it is sown a natural body, it is
> raised a spiritual body.[¶]

Here's a chart that illustrates the contrast between our present bodies and our kingdom bodies (all of this is consistent with Jesus's resurrection-body experience):

Our Present Bodies	Our Kingdom Bodies
Perishable	Imperishable
Dishonorable	Glorious
Weak	Powerful
Natural	Spiritual

---

[*] Luke 24:13–35
[†] John 21:13. Some suggest Jesus did not eat, but Luke 24:43 proves he did.
[‡] Luke 24:39; John 20:20
[§] John 20:19
[¶] 1 Corinthians 15:42–44

Notice that the word *spiritual* cannot mean "disembodied, spirit-y, soul-ishness." It must mean "a body made for the perfectly Spirit-driven world."

THAT BODY, OUR HOPE

The center of the Heaven Promise is that Jesus was raised from the dead. This is the heart of God's promise and of our hope.

Josh Ross is a pastor in some dodgy parts of Memphis, where he has learned about the scars that life, death, and violence can bring. But closer to home for Josh is a scar from the battle his older sister, Jenny, had to fight.

A text that Jenny sent to her parents on February 3, 2010, informed them that her temperature had spiked to 105. The next morning, Jenny, a mother and wife, was in the ICU with Group A Strep. By the time she had reached the emergency room, she "was in a full-blown battle with septic shock." Josh flew to Dallas, where a doctor told him: "There's a fifty/fifty chance." All Josh could do was stand by his sister's bed and cry and pray. In fact, a praying movement was ignited. Josh recorded his biggest questions from that day: "Why should a husband lose his wife? Why should my nine-year-old niece live the rest of her life without her mom?"

Jenny's infection required that drastic measures be taken in an attempt to save her life. "We thought the day they amputated her legs was the worst day of all." Josh continues: "The struggle lasted for eighteen days. We had been told that there was a one in five hundred thousand chance that sepsis would go to her brain."

"On February 22, 2010, we received the news that it had happened." Sepsis to the brain means death. "After my brother-in-law removed a lock of Jenny's hair, my family was excused from the room. . . . A doctor sang the ancient hymn . . . 'It Is Well'. . . . David lost his wife. Malaya lost her mom. My parents lost their only daughter. Jonathan and I lost our sister. The world lost a friend and a devout follower of Jesus."[7]

But Josh did not end the story there. He wrote about how the family faced death:

My dad tells the story of walking out of the hospital with my mom, knowing that at the age of fifty-three and fifty-two they had outlived their oldest child. They approached the sliding glass doors leading not just to a parking lot, but to a life they had never known before. There would not be a "normal" anymore. They each walked with a limp, because the lifelong journey of grief was setting in. My mom looked at my dad and said, "Remind me what we believe. What do we believe?"

After a few moments, my dad responded with these words: "The tomb is empty. The tomb is empty."[8]

Belief in the resurrection of Jesus as the first body fit for heaven matters in the here and now. Let's look back at the Chris and Stefanie Spielman story. What perhaps impressed the most people is how Stefanie led her life, even as the emperor of all maladies furtively but viciously ruled her life. When Stefanie's cancer had rendered her balance a serious problem, she obtained a three-wheel bicycle. One day she went for a ride through the neighborhood. A neighbor watched her and wrote a letter to Stefanie's sister, Sue, who walked alongside Stefanie on the ride:

Emotion flooded as I watched the two of you. . . . I felt sad, while the picture was so beautiful to me. . . . [We] are so grateful to God to know you and Stef, your husbands and your family. For us, you live as people from another planet, citizens of "no ordinary country," a glorious thing to see.[9]

One of the top reviews for Chris Spielman's book is by Sharon van der Walde, who volunteered alongside Stefanie in caring for cancer victims:

I remember when our oldest daughter (now 20) was about 9 or 10 and we were talking about Stef one night before bed and she said to me, "Mom, I think Mrs. Spielman is an angel and was put here on this earth to help others and when her job is done, she will return to heaven." She was right.[10]

Everything about life and death and heaven depends on one momentous event, nearly two thousand years ago, when—to use the magnificent imagery of C. S. Lewis in *The Lion, the Witch and the Wardrobe*—the Stone Table cracked,[11] death met its match, and one solitary figure, Son of God and Son of Man, got up and walked out of death's chilly fog on his own power, raised from the dead. The body of the resurrected Son of God is what heaven promises to each of us. In fact, each of us can learn to face death knowing that mists of that chilly fog are coming to an end.

Heaven: In Heaven or on Earth?

Is It Far Off and in the Future, or Right Now and on Earth?

> One day the curtain will be drawn back.
>
> — N. T. Wright

> God never gave up on his original plan for
> human beings to dwell on Earth.
>
> — Randy Alcorn

There is no mystery about the location of heaven.

Even more, the location of heaven shapes how we understand the Heaven Promise. I admit that in the past, I felt I knew where heaven is: the back nine, in the evening as the dew begins to rise and the sun is setting behind tall oaks, late summer, or at Pine Meadow Golf Club in the northern suburbs of Chicago. Joking aside, can we know where heaven is and will be? Yes, we really can.

MAPS OF PARADISE

The world-renowned historian Alessandro Scafi, in his book *Maps of Paradise*, maps the location of heaven through the history of Christian thinking.[1] Many

Christians have believed paradise was somewhere on earth, surely in some remote, forgotten, not-yet-found location. But still on earth. They reasoned that Adam and Eve were in paradise (the Garden of Eden), and that garden was connected to known rivers. If the Garden of Eden is paradise and heaven is paradise, then heaven is somewhere on this planet. In the famous *mappa mundi* in England's Hereford Cathedral, paradise was depicted as a walled garden on a remote island at the edge of the earth.

Here is Scafi's description of paradise, or heaven, as found on a famous medieval map of the world, the Ebstorf world map.[2] This map locates the Garden of Eden beyond India near the outer ocean, a body of water believed to have surrounded the world.

> The Garden of Eden is represented at the top of the map by a rectangle.
> Enclosed within it are Adam and Eve, the four rivers (shown disappearing
> into the ground), the Tree of Life and the Tree of the Knowledge of Good
> and Evil. . . . Eden is the first region of Asia . . . and is surrounded by a wall
> of fire that reaches up to heaven. The four great rivers of the earth have their
> origins in paradise and, after flowing below the surface of the earth, they
> reappear in different regions.[3]

As cartographers grew in their knowledge of a world where paradise could not be found, paradise, or heaven, was thought to occupy an invisible region/space. No one found paradise on earth. Nor will they. But this has not prevented Christians from searching and imagining where heaven might be.

So what are we to make of descriptions found in the book of Revelation? Based on the words of Revelation, some have constructed a map of heaven that shows God in the middle, high and lifted up on a Throne.[4] Behind God are myriad angels; before him and facing God are the twenty-four elders; to one side of God is a multitude of (perhaps 144,000) Israelites. To the other side is a multitude of celibates, and facing God opposite the angels are multitudes and multitudes of men and women.

Is that heaven? Where will it be? The book of Revelation says it is located in a place called "the new Jerusalem."* Does that mean heaven is Jerusalem? Maybe other map makers were just looking in the wrong place!

Up There, Out There, Heaven Above

The Bible points to a different location when it uses the term "heaven" or "heavens" . . . over *six hundred* times. God is shown speaking to humanity "from heaven." It is suggested that God dwells in the heavens and they are somewhere up there, or at least out there. Thus, "God heard the boy crying, and the angel of God called to Hagar from heaven and said to her." Or, "the angel of the Lord called out to him from heaven."† One could multiply such references a hundredfold. Furthermore, in the ancient world, the term *heaven* often referred to the sky.

One more point: heaven was understood to have layers upon layers, which is a likely explanation for why the Bible often speaks of "heavens," as in "God created the heavens and the earth" or "The Lord will open the heavens" or "The heavens praise your wonders, Lord" or "Those who are wise will shine like the brightness of the heavens." Jesus often spoke of the kingdom of *"heavens,"* a Jewish way of emphasizing the majesty of God over the entire cosmos.‡

So where is heaven? Is it up there or out there, or is it (in the future) to be found in Jerusalem?

Let's start with a safe and wise observation. Heaven is the place where God dwells. Since God is over and above all, any suggestion that God is up above or out there is just a way of speaking of God's glorious rule over all. If God is everywhere, then maybe heaven is everywhere God is—which is pretty close to saying everywhere.

If we combine the mapmakers' heaven and the up-there heaven, we might say there also is an earthy kind of heaven and a heavenly, spirit-y kind of heaven. Which is the real one?

Bear with me for one more important observation about how the Bible talks about heaven, but this observation will reshape the rest of this book.

---

* Revelation 21:2
† Genesis 21:17; 22:11
‡ Genesis 1:1; Deuteronomy 28:12; Psalm 89:5; Daniel 12:3; compare Matthew 4:17 could be "heavens" instead of "heaven."

THE BIBLE'S OWN HISTORY
OF THE LOCATIONS OF HEAVEN

The Bible speaks of heaven as a *temporary* place. N. T. Wright has written that "heaven is not a place in our space-time continuum, but a different sphere of reality that overlaps and interlocks with our sphere. . . . One day the curtain will be pulled back."[5] Randy Alcorn, whose life specialty is studying heaven, has written about two heavens: an "intermediate [present] Heaven" and the "new heavens and the New Earth."[6] Wright and Alcorn teach that *the present heaven is a temporary condition* and will give way to the fullness of heaven called the "new heavens and the new earth."

Here is the big point: We need to learn to talk about heaven in two phases or dimensions. They are the first heaven (now) and the final Heaven (the final kingdom of God). From this point on I will use lowercase *heaven* for the first heaven and uppercase *Heaven* for the final kingdom. The first heaven is real and present but *undisclosed* to mortal eyes, while the final Heaven is the *full disclosure* of the heavenly realm. And it will be *on a renewed earth*.

The history of heaven comes to light in the Bible in the form of two chapters. First is the undisclosed, hidden reality of the presence of God (first heaven). The second is the disclosed, visible reality of the presence of God on earth (final Heaven). The answer to the question "Where is heaven?" is that heaven occupies two locations. One is the undisclosed reality of God's presence, a reality more real than our lives now. The other location is the future new Heavens and new earth.

WHERE DO WE GO WHEN WE DIE?

Any discussion of Heaven can quickly get theoretical. But it also is deeply personal, since everyone who has reached adulthood eventually loses someone important to them. One of our most common questions is: What happened to my loved one when she died? Where did she go? The Bible's answer is that she went into the first heaven, which can be compared to dormitory life.

My dorm room at Cornerstone University in Grand Rapids contained four beds. I had three roommates, so four guys shared one small room with two closets and two desks. To shave and shower, everyone on the hall headed to a communal bathroom. We were finally free to live away from our parents, but in doing so we were constrained by cramped quarters. One roommate went home every weekend, in part to get more space, but also to see his girlfriend. God and earth be praised, dorm life doesn't last forever. A percentage of dorm residents graduate and move into an apartment or condo with the aim, in most cases, of eventually moving into a house.

I suggest that going to the first heaven and then to the final Heaven is like a student who moves from a dormitory into a condo or a home: we will move from heaven into Heaven.

WHAT ABOUT THE BODY?

It's natural to wonder what your body will be like between death and the kingdom. A careful study of Scripture indicates that we will go through three phases of existence. In one letter, Paul described all three phases of our existence. In Paul's second letter to the Christians living in Corinth,* he described our present life, which I'll call *Life Now,* as living in an earthly tent. Then he wrote about the *first heaven,* after death and prior to our resurrection, as being "unclothed" and "naked." Then he described the *Final Heaven:* in the kingdom of God we will live in a "building" or an "eternal house in heaven" or a "heavenly dwelling" where we will be fully "clothed." This chart compares and contrasts the three phases of our existence:

Life Now	First heaven	Final Heaven
Earthly tent, in body	Unclothed	Eternal house, clothed
Away from the Lord	With the Lord in heaven	With the Lord in new Heavens, new earth

It's worth taking a closer look at phase two, the dormitory—what many refer to as the intermediate state between death and Heaven. This is what the Bible often refers to as "paradise."

---

* 2 Corinthians 5:1–10

Jesus: "Today you will be with me in *paradise.*"

Jesus: "There was a rich man . . . [and] a beggar named Lazarus. . . . The time
came when the beggar died and the angels carried him to *Abraham's side*
[or paradise]. The rich man also died. . . . [He went to dwell] in *Hades*
[the opposite of paradise]." . . .

But Stephen, full of the Holy Spirit, looked up to heaven [paradise] and saw
the glory of God, and Jesus standing at the right hand of God.

Paul: "And I know that this man [Paul himself] . . . was caught up to
paradise." *

One more point about the first heaven. The New Testament often refers to the
death-state as a kind of *sleep.* But it speaks of sleep not because we are unconscious
but because it is temporary, like living in a college dormitory. There's a charming
back-and-forth in the gospel of John about this.† Jesus's good friend, Lazarus, had
died. The disciples were confused when Jesus said, "Our friend Lazarus has fallen
asleep; but I am going there to wake him up." Knowing Lazarus had been sick, the
disciples thought Jesus should allow the sick man to rest because it could help with
the healing process. So Jesus told them that, no, he meant "Lazarus is dead." Jesus
and the disciples went to Lazarus's house, and Jesus raised him from the dead. Jesus
saw his friend's death as sleep, a place of rest in the presence of God.

. . . then home in the final Heaven.

What comes after this dormitory heaven? The Bible describes the final state, the
eternal state, as the new Heaven and the new earth. Heaven, as it were, opens up a
long, shiny, slippery slide. It tips and we slide from heaven into the new Heavens and
the new earth.

As we discussed already, the book of Revelation describes the final Heaven, the
final state of God's people of promise, as a new Heaven and a new earth:

Then I saw "a new heaven and a new earth": for the first heaven and the first
earth had passed away, and there was no longer any sea. I saw the Holy City,

---

* Luke 23:43; Luke 16:19–31 (excerpted); Acts 7:55; 2 Corinthians 5:1–10; 12:3–4
† John 11; 1 Thessalonians 4:13

the new Jerusalem, coming down out of heaven from God, prepared as a
bride beautifully dressed for her husband.[*]

The first heaven, where we go when we die, is not our eternal location. What is
eternal is the new Heavens and the new earth that will be located on (our new) earth,
centered around the new Jerusalem. To get the two locations of heaven firmly in
view, we need to get over our inherited spirit-y view of heaven. Here is the biblical
disclosure: the *final Heaven is a very earthy, physical, embodied Heaven.* It is not a
Heaven made for souls and spirits alone but for whole persons—souls, spirits, and
bodies. For resurrected bodies designed for the kingdom of God. We will evidently
need homes when we get there.

Jesus described the final Heaven as a place with multitudes of rooms:[†]

Do not let your hearts be troubled. You believe in God; believe
also in me. My Father's house has many *rooms;* if that were not so,
would I have told you that I am going there to prepare a place for
you?

The word *rooms* was used in Jesus's world to refer to dwelling places for the
saints in God's presence. For instance, in Luke's gospel we read "you will be welcomed into eternal dwellings."[‡] A number of Jewish texts referred to heavenly "shel-
ters" or "chambers" in heaven for the faithful. But even more important is Revelation
21–22, where the new Heavens and the new earth are said to be a new city with
homes for the people of God. The important points from Jesus's words just quoted
are two: first, Jesus has prepared a dwelling place for each of us, and there are many,
many such dwellings for God's people.

The journey will be over when we get home, and home in God's order of promises is Heaven.

---

* Revelation 21:1–2
† John 14:1–2
‡ Luke 16:9

WE ARE ON A JOURNEY

Your life is a journey. God has invited you into the story of stories that takes place here before journeying to Heaven. When you get there you will, like a puzzle piece, suddenly see your place in God's adventure. In J. R. R. Tolkien's priceless story of the man named Niggle whose life passion was painting leaves, Niggle was too distracted ever to paint the whole tree. He was never satisfied with the leaves, even after laboring over them. He died without completing his mission: to paint the tree.

When he arrived in the final Heaven, he was given a bicycle, and Tolkien's priceless words create an image of what we will experience in the Heaven:

> Niggle pushed open the gate, jumped on the bicycle, and went bowling downhill in the spring sunshine. . . . Before him stood the Tree, his Tree, finished. . . . He went on looking at the Tree. All the leaves he had ever labored at were there, as he had imagined them rather than as he had made them; and there were others that had only budded in his mind, and many that might have budded, if only he had had time.[7]

You may think of yourself as having a relentlessly humdrum life, but when you get to Heaven, you will see where your own beauty fits in God's marvelous canvas.

SO WHERE IS IT?

I have not yet answered the question from the beginning of this chapter: Where is heaven? The book of Revelation tells us heaven and earth join one another to form the new Heavens and the new earth. This is described as the new Jerusalem, but where is that?

The Bible says the new Jerusalem is right here. Some believe the new Heavens and new earth will be located in the Middle East. (We can all hope the summer weather gets cooler.) This view has the new Heavens settling smack dab over top of Jerusalem, with God dwelling in the reconstructed temple.

But such an interpretation is too literal. The Bible doesn't say "Jerusalem" but "*new* Jerusalem." Like the body of Jesus after his resurrection, which again cannot be emphasized enough, and like our bodies, the new Heavens and the new earth will be completely *transformed but recognizable*. It will be a world that is similar to earth, but at the same time it will not be the earth. The new Heavens and the new earth will be a city *transformed* in a world *transformed* for the people of God *transformed*. It's right here, but it will all be brand-new.

These four elements shape everything about Heaven:

1. Heaven is a promise.
2. Everything about this promise depends on Jesus's resurrection.
3. In Heaven we will have resurrected bodies.
4. We will have embodied lives in the new Heavens and earth.

These four elements of God's sure promise bring us to Heaven, or the new Heavens and the new earth, our eternal home. All of this gives us the courage to face death by standing in Jesus's empty tomb—and standing on the Heaven Promise.

Facing Death Standing
in the Empty Tomb

Learning from Those Who Have Gone Before Us

[I pray] that you would have a rich life of joy and power,
abundant in supernatural results, with a constant clear
vision of never-ending life in God's world before you, and
the everlasting significance of your work day by day, a
radiant life and a radiant death.

— Dallas Willard

Many of us would like to script our own death scene, or at least we'd like to die on our own terms. We'd prefer a good death with family and friends surrounding us, offering the perfect word at the last moment. I know of no statistics on how many people experience this kind of parting, but my suspicion is that the numbers are very low.

Indeed, many face the prospect of death in fear; others offer trite words to allay such fears. Dietrich Bonhoeffer had been incarcerated in Tegel prison for almost a year. While there, through his brilliant, sensitive, and pastorally gifted eyes, he observed his fellow prisoners. On March 10, 1944, he wrote a letter to his best friend,

Eberhard Bethge, telling how fellow prisoners were facing their fear of nightly bombing raids that could bring sudden death to any of them. Bonhoeffer had seen and heard three basic ways that prisoners were facing the threatening nights. One group said, "Keep your fingers crossed for me." Another group said, "Touch wood," while a third group offered the bleaker assessment of "No one can avoid his fate." But Pastor Bonhoeffer wrote to Pastor Bethge these sad, gloomy words: "What I don't see at all is any relic of an eschatological sort."[1] Which is to say, none were putting their hope in the resurrection or in the Heaven Promise that sustained Bonhoeffer himself.

There is a way to die that I call "standing in the empty tomb" upon the promise of the resurrection and looking forward into the great beyond with hope. We have noble examples in those who have faced death in just such a hope.

JESUS

The death of Jesus, however tragic, reveals a man totally in control as he entered into those tender interiors.[2]

- He prayed for forgiveness for others: "Father, forgive them."
- He promised the thief they would be together that day in paradise.
- He provided for his mother: "Here is your son."
- He pleaded for drink: "I am thirsty."
- He publicized his accomplishment: "It is finished!"
- He pledged himself to the Father: "Into your hands I commit my spirit."

Dying in a gruesome fashion, Jesus still was in control. He knew he would be raised from the dead, so at his crucifixion he faced death, even as he kept in view the empty tomb.

DIETRICH BONHOEFFER

After months of a reasonably peaceful imprisonment, it was discovered that Dietrich Bonhoeffer was connected with a conspiracy to rid Germany of Hitler.[3] Hitler personally ordered the execution of the conspirators. All attempted communication to Bonhoeffer was shut down, family members lost contact with him, and interrogations increased. He was tortured and transported from prison to concentration camps designed for extermination. On the day before he was executed in the Flossenbürg concentration camp, Bonhoeffer and others were gathered in an abandoned schoolhouse in Schönberg to celebrate Easter the Sunday after the actual holiday. Most of those gathered were Roman Catholics, but they asked Pastor Bonhoeffer to lead a worship service.

Bonhoeffer used his daily Bible reading book. The texts for that day began with Isaiah 53:5, which read, "With his wounds we are healed." Surely they realized Jesus was the pioneer into their own suffering, and surely they sought assurance from his atoning death. Then they turned to the next reading, 1 Peter 1:3: "Blessed be the God and Father of our Lord Jesus Christ! By his great mercy we have been born anew to a living hope." The final word that day was not death; the final word was new life through the resurrection.

Standing in the empty tomb of Jesus having celebrated Easter, Dietrich Bonhoeffer faced a hideous execution the next day. When two civilians came for him, they announced, "Prisoner Bonhoeffer, get ready and come with us!" The Englishman Payne Best was with the prisoners when Bonhoeffer was taken, attesting that Bonhoeffer approached him in a calm demeanor and asked him to tell Bishop Bell of Chichester that "This is the end—for me the beginning of life."

CHRISTIAN WIMAN'S GRANDMOTHER

Christian Wiman's grandmother was another individual who stood boldly in the empty tomb. Wiman, a cancer-stricken American poet with a piercing faith, remembered fondly his grandmother and her witness. She lived, he said, in a house with "a million immaculate nooks, and museum stillnesses." One summer, Wiman spent his time reading and writing and visiting with his grandmother. She and her sister were so devout that "even their daily chores [were] accompanied by hymns hummed under their breath." He offers these words of hope-inducing faith about his grandmother's passing: "that her every tear was wiped away, that God looked her out of pain, that in the blink of an eye the world opened its tenderest interiors, and let her in."[4] Both Wiman and his grandmother faced her death with a courage and steadfastness that can only be attributed to a faith with roots in the empty tomb.

Dallas Willard

Some deaths send us onward with more courage and hope. Dallas Willard brought God's presence into every setting. Though his death darkened the day for all who heard of his passing, his life told a story of hope and heaven. Dallas stood for days in the empty tomb, waiting for his death's stone to be rolled away. His granddaughter, Larissa Heatley, said this at his funeral:

> And he also used to wave us off as we drove away. Now, some people will wave their family off for a little while, but he had a *long* driveway and he would wave goodbye to me from behind the white picket fence until we couldn't see each other anymore. He would do it every time, without fail. It became our way of saying "I love you, and see you soon" without having to say anything.
>
> "I love you, and see you soon" was the last thing I said to him. I will still see him soon in heaven. He told me in the hospital that if he passed, it wouldn't be long until we resumed our life together. . . .
>
> I will always remember one sentence that really summed up everything he stood for and everything I need to do. . . . We were all walking out of the [hospital] room and he called me back just for a moment so we were the only two in the room, and he said, "Give 'em Heaven."[5]

Prior to a class he taught, Dallas once prayed that each of the students would have a "radiant death."

Gary Black Jr. was to Dallas Willard what Mitch Albom was to Morrie, made famous in *Tuesdays with Morrie*. After spending long hours with Dallas, working to help complete some of Dallas's writing projects, Gary was in the room when Dallas died. Here is his reflection:

After the family left, I must have fallen asleep again and awoke at 4:30 am when a nurse came in to turn him. When she did, he awoke briefly. I took his hand. He told me to tell his loved ones how much he was blessed by them, how much he appreciated them and that he would be waiting for them when they arrive. I assured him I would . . . There was joy in his eyes. Something had changed. Or something was about to change.

I then told him the nurse was ready to administer some more medicine and he was going to go back to sleep. I told him I thought this time he might not wake up. I asked him if that was what he wanted. He said yes with a slight but distinct little grin. I looked up at the nurse. She heard his words and increased the pain medication. I kissed him on the forehead and said goodbye one last time. He closed his eyes and smiled. I sat back in the chair next to his bedside and watched him take maybe 10 quiet breaths. There was no sign of pain on his face. No hiccups, no cramping, no waves of teeth-grinding agony, no coughing. Just peaceful rest. Then, in a voice clearer than I had heard in days, he leaned his head back slightly and with his eyes closed said, "Thank You."[6]

Some die with memorable words describing their entrance into the very presence of God. This was the case with John Wesley, who said twice, "The best of all is God is with us."[7] The same is true of D. L. Moody. J. Wilbur Chapman, one of his biographers, records these final words of Moody's:

Is this dying? Why this is bliss.
There is no valley. I have been within the gates.
Earth is receding; Heaven is opening; God is calling; I must go.[8]

Some seem to die in a fit of joy, as Gerard Manly Hopkins, the famous poet did, saying, "I am so happy, I am so happy."[9] But not everyone dies in a state of joy or certainty. William Wilberforce, a man of great faith, died with words that express hope. Eric Metaxas, in his biography of Wilberforce, wrote that in great physical pain, he uttered his last words:

Barbara and his youngest, Henry, were with him that night when he stirred
one last time. "I am in a very distressed state," he said. "Yes," Henry said, "but
you have your feet on the Rock." The man whose voice and words had
changed the world now spoke his last. "I do not venture to speak so positively," he said. "But I hope I have."[10]

We might hope that we would all have such serene last moments; sadly our
fallen world does not always permit it to be so. Thankfully Jesus rose from the dead.
The empty tomb empowers us to look death in the eye and announce that victory is
coming shortly.

We can do this because the Heaven Promise teaches us to see the promise of God
as we stand in the empty tomb. In fact, that Heaven Promise is so full it can be split
into six promises. As we turn now to what God promises, we are in need of a special
warning. I want to stick with the big ideas about (the final) Heaven and avoid speculation as much as possible. If we can learn to think about the big ideas—these six
promises we are about to discuss—we will be much further along the path of thinking about Heaven as it actually is. If, however, we opt too quickly for the imaginations of the imaginative, we are likely to start thinking about Heaven in ways that
simply won't square with what the Bible says.

Now to the six big promises about Heaven.

Part Three

GOD'S SIX PROMISES ABOUT HEAVEN

Imaginations run ahead of the Bible far too often when we discuss the kingdom, Heaven. Will we know our friends? Will we be married? Will there be pets?

Before we can attempt to answer questions like these, we need to get the big ideas about Heaven sorted out.

These are the big ideas about the Heaven Promise as found in the Bible:

First Promise: God Will Be God

Second Promise: Jesus Will Be Jesus

Third Promise: Heaven Will Be the Utopia of Pleasures

Fourth Promise: Heaven Will Be Eternal Life

Fifth Promise: Heaven Will Be an Eternal Global Fellowship

Sixth Promise: Heaven Will Be an Eternal Beloved Community

After a discussion of each, we turn to the first hour in Heaven and answer the question, What will it be like?

The First Promise: God Will Be God

> He shall be the end of our desires who shall be seen without
> end, loved without cloy, praised without weariness.
>
> — St. Augustine

Some believe in the final Heaven but think we can know very little about it. After all, if the Bible reveals only snapshots or, perhaps even better, Monet-like impressions, what can *we* know about it?

I'll answer that challenge-like question by probing what the general impressions actually tell us about Heaven. If we reduce our imaginations even to simple notes and omit the riffs and resonances, what then will the final Heaven be like? Gary Scott Smith, who wrote an academic history on how Americans have understood Heaven, provides almost a complete listing of the big ideas about Heaven in a series of questions, questions you might want to answer for yourself:

1. Is it a place of continuous worship or a perpetual playground?
2. Is it a realm of eternal rest or of vigorous activity?
3. Is it a site of static perfection or of everlasting progress?
4. Is it an exhilarating, enchanting paradise or a boring, dull place?[1]

If we take a good look at Heaven in the Bible, what are the most important features?

The first nonnegotiable feature of the Heaven Promise has to do with God. In Heaven, God will be God. Sketches of Heaven begin well when they begin with

God—on the Throne, in the Center of all centers, the Star of all stars, the Light of all lights, and the Glory of all of Heaven's many glories. Which leads you and me to a rather obvious conclusion: *Heaven is designed for and only comfortable for God-lovers.*

God shapes Heaven for those who delight in him so much they want to dwell in his presence and gaze upon his ever-expanding beauty all eternity long. It is not selfish on God's part to be glorified; it is right and good. In fact, it is gracious of God to grant us such endless basking in his love. If God really is God, then Heaven will be when God will be fully God to everyone and everything.

FACE TIME WITH GOD

When I was a teenager, a member of the military visited my hometown while on leave from the Vietnam War. He was a pilot, and he buzzed our city. He was not flying a Cessna. He had gone AWOL with a military jet, flying over our city of Freeport, Illinois, at a dangerously low altitude. I was outside at the time, and that plane scared me to death. I ran under the garage cover, which wasn't much protection, to hide from what I feared might be the rapture or something worse. (I was told later the pilot got in some deep trouble.)

The sound—and here's my point—scared me so deeply that it wouldn't be accurate to say it stopped at the bone. It made me feel like I was coming apart at the cell level. God's own glory has the same terrifying impact on humans who, because of sin and mortality, cannot endure the full presence of that kind of barrier-cracking light, sound, power, majesty, and sheer transcendence.

Because God's presence is unendurable for humans, the narrative of Scripture does not always make sense as we are reading and living it. However, it becomes clear at the very end. It is the story of Peniel, the story of seeing God face to face. Sometimes God seems to pull back the curtains of the first heaven to buzz humans so they can see God face to face. But other times the Bible says very explicitly that humans cannot gaze into the face of God and *survive the glorious brilliance and glory and weight of God's own face.*

I believe God's full presence is unendurable for humans in the here and now, but at the end of history, we all will have face time with God. We won't merely endure God's glorious presence—it will be our greatest joy. So here's a brief glimpse of the Bible's story of face time with God.*

Jacob wrestled with God and was wounded, but he survived. He called the place *Peniel,* which is Hebrew for "the face of God."

Moses, on the other hand, hid his face from God because he was afraid to look at God. Sometime later God explicitly revealed to Moses that he could not see God's face but he could see his "back," which means the back of the face of God. But the same book, Exodus, also tells us that Moses sometimes spoke with God "face to face." If you're confused, so is everyone else, and we are probably confused because the Bible is using language that cannot describe the awe, beauty, majesty, and unapproachableness of God as God approaches us! What we do learn about Moses is that his face-to-face time with God created such a divine sunburn of glorious brightness on his face that he had to wear a veil.

David evidently didn't see God face to face, but he longed to: "One thing I ask from the Lord, this only do I seek: . . . to gaze on the beauty of the Lord and to seek him in his temple."†

Isaiah and Ezekiel both were buzzed with visions of God, but it is not until Jesus that we all encounter God face to face. Jesus is Immanuel, "God with us." Surely inspired by having seen Jesus transfigured on the mountain, the apostle John wrote these words:

> The Word became flesh and made his dwelling among us. We have seen his glory, the glory of the one and only Son, who came from the Father, full of grace and truth.

John clarified the Bible's story of face time with God by pointing out that *no one in human history,* not Jacob, not Moses, not Isaiah, and not Ezekiel, had seen God. Here are John's words:

---

* See Genesis 32:30; Exodus 3:6; 33:11, 20, 23; 34:35; Isaiah 6; Ezekiel 1; Matthew 1:23; 17:1–9; John 1:14, 18; Revelation 1:12–18; 22:4
† Psalm 27:4

No one has ever seen God, but the one and only Son, who is himself God
and is in closest relationship with the Father, has made him known.

So, when it comes to actual face time, no one saw God until they saw Jesus,
who fills in the face of Peniel. On earth, Jesus once transfigured himself before
his chosen disciples to manifest his essential glory—the resurrection body. And
the book of Revelation opens with John catching a glimpse of this same glorious
Jesus.

But the face-time problem humans have with taking in the unbearable glory of
God ends in the final Heaven. John promised that we "will see his face, and his name
will be on [our] foreheads."* Paul gave us the same promise: "For now we see only a
reflection as in a mirror; then we shall see face to face."†

MAGIC EYES

What happens to a human in God's presence? Or to use an older term, can we *abide*
God's presence? How can we endure the immensity, the infinity, the brilliant gaze
and numinous presence of the One behind, over, through, and under it all? Surely
we have to be transformed to abide in the very presence of God.

When my children were young they had Magic Eye books that contained au-
tostereogram. I'm sure you have seen these books. Here's my attempt at a definition:
you stare at a bundle of dots and the dots morph into a three-dimensional picture,
and all the while you lose peripheral vision. This means you kind of enter into that
picture. Somehow our eyes adjust and are transformed for the image, then it is as if
we enter into the scene.

Being with God will be like that, only to a far greater degree! Our ordinary life
of devotion to God, which we experience on a spectrum from wonderful to less than
wonderful, is like that bundle of dots. When we encounter God fully under the
power of a transformed body—very similar to Jesus's resurrection body—the dots
will suddenly be seen through a deeper experience of life. At that moment, all the

---

* Revelation 22:4
† 1 Corinthians 13:12; see also 1 John 3:2

dots suddenly will make sense. Most importantly, we will become absorbed with the depth of who God is.

God will dwell with us, and we will dwell with God. That's the Heaven Promise. But when we get that close to God, transformation is inevitable because God's deep glory will remain an unapproachable light. Jeffrey Burton Russell calls our heavenly union with God a "fiery proximity."[2] We will encounter God's weighty presence as a fiery proximity, and we will be transformed to delight in that fire. St. John of the Cross spoke of God's presence as the "living flame of love."[3] Russell and St. John of the Cross together have the right idea: our mutual dwelling with God will be a fiery and intimate love. But one thing is clear: we are not yet ready for that depth of union.

People who have learned to know God, who have practiced a life of spending time with God, are the people who long to see God face to face. If you have ever yearned to catch but a glimpse of God's glory, the way Jacob and Moses and Isaiah and Ezekiel and the apostles on the mountain glimpsed it, you can know for certain that day is coming. God graciously stays beyond and behind the veil now, but only for our own safety. Someday, the veil will be torn away and we will have the capacity to see God and endure it. But not just endure it. We will long for it and enjoy it endlessly.

Heaven is for those who long to gaze upon the beautiful face of God.

GOD WILL BE "ALL IN ALL"

The apostle Paul brushed up against the end of all history in describing the coming of the kingdom of God.* How will it unfold? First the resurrection of Jesus, then at his return Jesus will triumph over the powers of evil at work in the world. And then he will conquer death itself before he hands over the kingdom to the Father. This Son-to-Father exchange will be accompanied by a big thunderclap of praise that announces, "Mission accomplished!" Paul concludes this account with an ear-bending expression: "so that God may be all in all." That's the end and goal of all of history and what we were made to enjoy the most.

In one of his most famous prayers, John Henry Newman turned this "all in all"

---

* 1 Corinthians 15:20–28

theme into the notion that we will be so enthralled with God that we will be "dissolved" in God: "It is the occupation of eternity, ever new, inexhaustible, ineffably ecstatic . . . thus to drink in and be dissolved in Thee."[4]

In Heaven God will be all in all. Here are some indications of how central and all-focused God will be in Heaven.

- *God will make all things new.* The One on the Throne, that is, God, declares for all to hear. "*I* am making everything new!'"*
- *God is the origin and the goal.* Then the same God says, "*I* am the Alpha and the Omega," which can only mean one thing: God is the beginning and the end of all existence and the center of the meaning of it all.
- *God will make the Bible's central promise good.* God says, "*I* will be their God and they will be my children."†
- Here was a shocker for first-century Jews: John revealed there would be *no temple in the final Heaven.* Why? "Because the Lord God Almighty and the Lamb *are* its temple."‡ The temple pointed all worshipers to God. When God becomes altogether present, there will be no need for the pointer.
- *God will be the light.* No sun or moon from celestial lights. Why? "For the glory of God gives it light, and the Lamb is its lamp."§
- *God will be the sustenance for all.* The water of life and the tree of life that sustain the life of kingdom people are "flowing from the throne of God and of the Lamb."¶

We find here a potent critique of the life we now lead. What is central for us in the here and now will be decentralized, and the One who is now decentralized will be centralized. What is central, say, in our nation? If you let news stories shape your sense of what is important, you will learn that it all happens in Washington, DC, on Capitol Hill and in the White House. And that means much of it happens in backrooms where the people of power meet to make decisions that shape our lives.

---

* Revelation 21:5
† Revelation 21:6–7
‡ Revelation 21:22
§ Revelation 21:23
¶ Revelation 22:1

Or we are influenced to believe that it all happens on Wall Street, where folks with the funds meet to decide. Or in our state's capital or in our community's town hall. Or it happens in meetings at church or over coffee with those who broker the power. Or in your home or neighborhood or down at the baseball stadium.

These things are central to us now, but they all will be decentralized. Consider that John included not one word about any of these earthly attachments as he set forth Revelation's grand vision. Instead, at the center are God and the Lamb. Humans encircle God in prayer and praise and worship and celebration and fellowship. The humans of Heaven live out an existence utterly centered on God.

No writer has captured God's centrality in Heaven better than Augustine. He imagined someone wondering about life in Heaven: "What will I do [in Heaven]? There will be no work for our limbs; what, then, will I do?" He then said he would answer: "Is this no activity: to stand, to see, to love, to praise [God]?"[5] For Augustine the central theme of Heaven is to worship God endlessly. As J. I. Packer once put it, "The hearts of those in heaven say, 'I want this to go on forever.' And it will."[6]

One of the most stimulating dimensions of the Heaven Promise is the realization that all creation will be centered on our God, the All in All.

ALL CREATION UNLOOSED

Though not prominent in any scene about Heaven in the Bible, all of creation will be set free and will turn to God in praise.* We return to the resurrection body of Jesus. As the resurrection body magnified into glory Jesus's earthly body, so *the new Heavens and the new earth will magnify into glory what we see in the heavens and the earth now.* Which is to say: creation itself will experience God's full salvation to become the creation it was designed to become. The new Heavens and the new earth are the old heavens and the old earth redeemed, restored, and renewed into the form they will have forever and ever.

God created this world to magnify God, and he placed us on earth to govern this world as God's stewards. This means that at the core of God's design of us, we

---

* Romans 8:21

have an *ecological or creation mandate.* We were not created to exploit this earth but to enhance it, nurture it, sustain it, and protect it. Rivers and lakes and oceans, mountains and canyons and flatlands, gardens of fruits and vegetables, and fields of grasses and animals good for food. We were created to nurture and to offer these as thanksgiving offerings to God.

We have sadly exploited all these things, but in Heaven the rivers will flow with healthy drinking and cooking water, and the fields will produce food without the incursion of thistles and thorns and weeds. Flatlands and mountains and oceans and rivers and every placid lake will reverberate with praise to God. And that same creation will sit in judgment on our exploitations. We will repent from our sins, and we will join with all creation in singing loud hosannas to the All in All. Forever and ever.

GETTING READY NOW FOR THE GOD OF HEAVEN

We gain glimpses of God as All in All when we commune with God in worship and prayer, and when we stand in nature and look up to God. In prayer we often attempt to find God at the center of our thoughts and our lives. Sometimes we have to discipline ourselves to discover that thin place where we sense we are communing with God. This discipline is called "recollection." As Richard Foster described: "It means a simple recollecting* of ourselves until we are unified or whole. . . . The idea is to let go of all competing distractions until we are truly present where we are."[7] Recollection ushers us into quiet, and quiet can lead us into the experience of God's pulsating, interactive love.

Heaven will end the need for us to muster our energies into recollection. Why? Because God will be ever present, and we will be ever present to God. Heaven means constant ecstasy because recollection and quiet will be constant graces. In our lives on earth, we enter and leave the ecstasy of engagement with God, but in Heaven we will dwell in that engagement.

As we work,

as we converse,

---

* It might help to see the pronunciation: not "wreck-a-lecting" but "ree-collecting."

as we serve, and

as we carry on with the routine life of Heaven . . .

. . . we will be fully engaged in the very presence of God. We will at all times carry with us the experience of God's presence. In this world we carry some bit of great news—a new job, a raise, the announcement of a new grandchild—for a bubbly day or two. In Heaven, the bubbly joy of engagement with God will never cease.

As we learn the basic ideas of Heaven found in the Bible, we begin with this: in Heaven, God will be all in all. In addition, the more centered God becomes, the more we see Jesus, who is the second basic idea about the Heaven Promise.

The Second Promise:
Jesus Will Be Jesus

The kingdom of the world has become the kingdom of our
Lord and of his Messiah, and he will reign for ever and ever.

— The apostle John

I n the center of the biblical vision of heaven is God, but if you keep looking at
the God of Heaven, you'll notice that the images morph. On the throne in
Heaven is God. On the throne in Heaven is the Lamb. On the throne in Heaven
is the Lion of the tribe of Judah. Heaven is designed for people who love Jesus and
long to be with him forever and ever. As we will see shortly, those who long to be
with Jesus want to be with the Jesus who will conquer evil and death and create a
world of love and life.

One of the saddest moments of my teaching career was the day a college student
asked to meet after my Jesus class. We walked together to my office, sat down, and then
she looked at me with tears in her eyes. She said, "I've been to church all my life, and I
don't think I ever heard about Jesus. I love him and want to dedicate my life to him.
Why did I not hear about Jesus in church?" There are a lot of reasons: we get distracted
with programs and budgets and getting saved and going to heaven and mission trips
and choirs and bands and worship teams and elder board and committee meetings.

Far too often in our churches, *what* too easily replaces *who*. The who of Heaven is God and, as C. S. Lewis once said, anyone "who has God and everything else has no more than he who has God only."[1] As I mentioned, the who of Heaven morphs back and forth between God on the Throne and the Lamb on the Throne. In Heaven the who will be central.

IMAGINE HEARING THIS IN THE FIRST CENTURY

Listen to these stunning words of the apostle Paul, words that had to shock his first-century audience. Here we are exposed to an incomparable and incomprehensible exaltation of Jesus:

> The Son is the image of the invisible God, the firstborn over all creation. For in him all things were created: things in heaven and on earth, visible and invisible, whether thrones or powers or rulers or authorities; all things have been created through him and for him. He is before all things, and in him all things hold together. And he is the head of the body, the church; he is the beginning and the firstborn from among the dead, so that in everything he might have the supremacy. For God was pleased to have all his fullness dwell in him, and through him to reconcile to himself all things, whether things on earth or things in heaven, by making peace through his blood, shed on the cross.*

Imagine what it was like for a Jew such as Paul, that is, someone who believed in one God, to have written these lines. For Paul, Jesus is:

- The express manifestation of the invisible God
- The Creator of all
- That which all creation aims toward
- The Lord of the church

---

* Colossians 1:15–20

- The first One raised from among the dead
- The dwelling of God's complete fullness
- The One through whom God has reconciled all things

From the very beginning of the church, Paul and the earliest Christians were Jesus-centered. Their *who* was what the Father revealed in the Son.

The same is true in the last book of the Bible. From the beginning of Revelation to the end, the focus is twofold: God's Throne and Jesus the Lamb. Over and over and over it is about who. The Lamb lived and was slain, but he was raised to rule and to conquer evil. In the opening chapter of the book of Revelation, Jesus has an encounter with John:

Then he placed his right hand on me and said: "Do not be afraid. I am the
First and the Last. I am the Living One; I was dead, and now look, I am alive
for ever and ever! And I hold the keys of death and Hades.*

The mighty ruling God on the Throne has a scroll in his right hand and, after scanning all of creation, it is discovered that none dare approach the Throne to open the scroll. None, that is, but the Lamb:

Then one of the elders said to me, "Do not weep! See, the Lion of the tribe of
Judah, the Root of David, has triumphed. He is able to open the scroll and its
seven seals."†

When you consider these words in the context of the first century—taking into account geopolitical realities like the emperor in Rome, prevailing religious beliefs, and the power structure—the message will shake you even more. These words of Paul and John are striking, bold postures. To the Jews, Paul has said, in effect, God became incarnate in a human, Jesus. To the Romans, John has said: "The Lion of the tribe of Judah will reign," not Caesar. These are words of revolution. Their *who* was not a worldly emperor but the World's True Emperor.

---

* Revelation 1:17–18
† Revelation 5:5

THE LAMB WHO IS LION ON THE THRONE

If you follow the book of Revelation from beginning to end, you will notice a wonderful narrative about Jesus. Jesus reveals himself in full glory to John in the first chapter. Jesus at first is disclosed as the Lord of the churches. But that glorious figure morphs into a lamb who is slain in chapter 4. Then as you follow the plot, you see the lamb becoming a warrior, a lion* who also is a lamb. This lamb-lion triumphs over evil—over the beast and over Babylon.

What is perhaps most amazing, then, is the image chosen for Jesus in the New Jerusalem. In the final Heaven, Jesus is not the Lion of Judah, but instead the Lamb. Jesus is the one who was victorious by entering into enemy territory and storming the forces of evil. He won by giving his life and by being raised from the dead. If in chapter 4 of Revelation they praise the Lamb for being worthy, he is more worthy in the final Heaven because his work is finished. By then, all redemption is accomplished and the Lamb has relocated the Heaven people in their final home.

Jesus will be praised forever and beyond, the way kings are glorified after victories over enemies. Jesus's enemies are legion: Satan, evil spirits, diabolical rulers, corrupted systems. When he is paraded before the throngs of saints in glory, they will toss their glories onto his accomplishments. They will perhaps echo the song of Chris Tomlin about the splendor of the king before whom the whole world can rest in pleasured joy. We all will be in ceaseless praise at the greatness of God, and as Tomlin expresses it, "The Godhead Three in One, Father, Spirit and Son."[2] In keeping with what we read in Revelation, Tomlin gives a sequence to titles for Jesus. Lion precedes Lamb. The Lion who triumphed over enemies did so as the Lamb who was slain. The who of Heaven is the Lamb-who-is-the-Lion.

GOD'S TEAM WINS

My friend Randy Harris teaches at Abilene Christian University. He humorously reduces the message of the book of Revelation to just three lines:

---

* Revelation 5:5; 10:3

God's team wins

Choose your team

Don't be stupid!

I want to focus on the fact that God's team wins. If God will conquer all evil and establish a final, eternal justice and peace, and if God will rule over all, then we who are with God will be on the side of the ruling God.

Even if many in our world don't see it or if they demean the idea, the Bible teaches us that there is right now a cosmic battle going on between good and evil, a battle that is sometimes glimpsed in *Star Wars* or *The Lord of the Rings* or *Harry Potter* or *The Chronicles of Narnia's The Last Battle*. A major source of evil in our world is the "dragon, that ancient serpent, who is the devil, or Satan."* Satan has companions, and the word *companion* intentionally mocks the true meaning of the word. They are his companions as long as they do his bidding, and Satan's bidding is to bring people to death and to prevent them from finding life in God. As if to make the story even more dramatic, this source of evil will be locked up for a millennium of years only to be released one more time for his last assault on our brothers and sisters. After which reckless release, the devil will be tossed forever into the lake of fire.†

We dare not blame all evil on the devil, but it's at work in every instance of evil—from sex trafficking to the ruining of a life through drugs to sexual adulteries that destroy marriages and homes and propagate even more infidelities. The devil whispers in our ears that pleasures are good, that the job can wait, that money is to enjoy, that drink is to indulge in, that food is fine because we won't live forever . . . Each temptation is one more sprinkling of the dust of death tossed at us by the devil. But there will come a day when the serpent will be destroyed forever.

In Heaven we will see the victorious Conqueror on the throne, but his name will not be Caesar or Mr. President or Madame Prime Minister. His name is Jesus, and he will be the true paradox: the Lion of the tribe of Judah has become the Lamb who was slain. He will conquer all sin, evil, and injustice. Christ defeated the devil at the

---

* Revelation 20:2
† Revelation 20:10

cross, and death was reversed through the resurrection. But until heaven we are called to face the temptations of Satan and his deathly designs. The day is coming when the devil and his death will end.

Evil takes root in some humans, and then they become dealers of the devil's death, but those people will meet their end too. Here is the end of some who have ruined themselves:

> But the cowardly, the unbelieving, the vile, the murderers, the sexually immoral, those who practice magic arts, the idolaters and all liars . . .
>
> Nothing impure will ever enter it, nor will anyone who does what is shameful or deceitful. . . .
>
> Outside are the dogs, those who practice magic arts, the sexually immoral, the murderers, the idolaters and everyone who loves and practices falsehood.*

The Bible does not squeeze some sins while ignoring others. Instead, the Bible sees humans in whom evil has taken root. The focus is on how evil destroys what God most wants: confident faith, life, sexual fidelity, worship of the one true God, and most emphatically, truth telling.

"THE FAINT OUTLINE"

Even if sometimes the Lamb looks defeated, the victory will come. Malcolm Muggeridge, who had been raised practically an atheist and a socialist in England by radical parents, departed from England for the Soviet Union prior to World War II. He expected to find a utopian kingdom on earth in Stalin's Russia. As a journalist he ran up against the low-truth quotient that Soviet censors mandated in news reports. With his wife having just barely survived a brush with death in their home in Russia, he went on a ruminating walk through a forest. What he discovered in that forest was a church being used for political propaganda.

---

* Revelation 21:8, 27; 22:15

Peeping in through a broken window of the little church with the newly painted front, I saw that it was used now for storing tools, as well as some of the fallen [political] slogans from the nearby clearing.[3]

Sad but true, a church converted from worship to storage for political propaganda signs. But hear what Muggeridge saw beyond the signs:

Yet at the back where the altar had been there was still the *faint outline* of a cross to be seen. In its survival I read the promise that somehow this image of enlightenment [in Christ] through suffering, this assertion of the everlasting supremacy of the gospel of [God's] love over the gospel of [Stalin's] power, would never be obliterated, however dimly and obscurely traced now, and however seemingly triumphant the forces opposed to it might seem to be.[4]

The faint outline of a cross hidden behind the injustices of violence, when seen for its revealing message, announces, "THE LAMB WILL TRIUMPH!"

JESUS WILL BE JESUS

Who is Jesus? Jesus is God's Son, God's Messiah, God's Word, God's Savior. In the final Heaven, this victorious Jesus will be celebrated.

This is why in the new Heavens and the new earth, the Lamb is in the middle of everything. The language is metaphorical, but what it conveys is clear as a night sky filled with God's starry host. I am speaking of the language of Revelation 21:22—22:5. Take note of the centrality of Jesus (the Lamb) in Heaven:

I did not see a temple in the city, because the Lord God Almighty *and the Lamb are its temple.* The city does not need the sun or the moon to shine on it, for the glory of God gives it light, *and the Lamb is its lamp.* The nations will walk by its light, and the kings of the earth will bring their splendor into it. . . . Nothing impure will ever enter it, nor will anyone who does what is shameful or deceitful, but only those whose names are *written in the Lamb's book of life*.

Then the angel showed me the river of the water of life, as clear as crystal, flowing from the throne of God *and of the Lamb* down the middle of the great street of the city. . . . The throne of God *and of the Lamb* will be in the city, and his servants will serve him. They will see his face, and *his name will be on their foreheads*. There will be no more night. They will not need the light of a lamp or the light of the sun, for the Lord God will give them light. And they will reign for ever and ever.

Without taking away one speck of glitter of God's glory, the Lamb becomes central to everything in Heaven. The God of Heaven is seen most clearly in the Lamb and the Lamb is a reflection of the God of Heaven. Heaven is all about God and the Lamb.

We move now to a third fundamental promise of Heaven, this one about who will populate the final Heaven.

The Third Promise: Heaven Will Be the Utopia of Pleasures

> If I find in myself a desire which no experience in this
> world can satisfy, the most probable explanation is that I
> was made for another world. . . . There have been times
> when I think we do not desire heaven; but more often I find
> myself wondering whether, in our heart of hearts, we have
> ever desired anything else.
>
> — C. S. Lewis

We can be happy, we will be happy, we should be happy. We have a right to happiness." So says one of the best chroniclers of the human pursuit of happiness.[1]

Happiness, or at least the pursuit of happiness, is one reason America declared its independence. In fact, it's one of our "unalienable" rights. Happiness depends in part on one's age and in part on where we stack up to others in our perception of what's fair and right. What matters here is not so much the *right* or even how we get it, but this: *God wired us in such a way that happiness, or what I would rather call "deep joy," motivates our every move.*

Of course, at times this pursuit of happiness can be incredibly self-centered and self-preoccupied. But when we scatter our selfishness to the corners of existence, and if we are really honest, we all *yearn to be fully happy*. Not so much happy clappy with smiley-face tattoos, but possessing a deeply settled joy that brings peace and contentment in knowing who we are and where we fit in God's designs for the earth we inhabit.

Heaven is designed for those who want this deep joy. Dare we call Heaven a place of pleasure? Absolutely.

PLEASURE IN HEAVEN

We start with Saint Augustine: "It is the decided opinion of all who use their brains that all men desire to be happy."[2] For all of us now who want to use our brains with brainy Augustine, let's admit this truth: we want to be happy. The problem is that happiness is, to borrow and adapt a line, as happiness does. So what might happiness be?

As philosopher Stewart Goetz summarized it, "Perfect happiness . . . consists of nothing but conscious psychological states of . . . pleasure."[3] He's right: the word *happiness* belongs with the word *pleasure*. But we are taught somewhere and everywhere—by parents, by pastors and priests, by professionals—that pleasure is a lower good and that pursuit of pleasure is, well, hedonism. Not so fast. If we are wired by God's design to chase happiness with all our might, and if happiness cannot be separated from pleasure, then maybe we need a conversion of our imaginations. I make this claim: *all contemporary pleasures are designed by God to point us toward the final Heaven.* As C. S. Lewis said, "I [would] say that every pleasure (even the lowest) is a likeness to, even, in its restricted mode, a foretaste of the end for [which] we exist, the fruition [enjoyment] of God."[4]

Now to the stunning observation that we have all been waiting for: God dwells in endless pleasure and happiness and in deep joy. Our desire for deep joy comes from God's deep dwelling in God's own deep joy. God is a happy God; God is full of joy; God is all pleasure and designs all pleasure. Our enjoyment of pleasure is participating in God's own pleasure.

Again from C. S. Lewis: "God not only understands but *shares* . . . the desire for complete and ecstatic happiness." You may want to read that again: Lewis connected God with ecstasy. But those of us who have used our brains have a shared observation: no pleasure, no joy, no happiness on this earth fully satisfies. So once again, recalling the words of Lewis, "If I find in myself a desire which no experience in this world can satisfy, the most probable explanation is that I was made for another world."[5] That unsatisfied desire is the desire for the final Heaven's lasting, eternal, deep pleasure and joy.

Heaven is a world of happiness, a world of intense pleasures, a world of deep joy. Heaven is designed for people who yearn for that kind of happiness, that kind of pleasure, and that kind of deep joy. I'll say it: the thrills of intimate relationships among friends and family and societies, the sensual pleasures of orgasm, the inexpressible delight of perfectly pitched music for the perfect moment, the rich fullness of a rose's fragrance enhanced by wafts of freshly mowed grass, the sensory touches of skin and shape and form, the glories of a sunset, the intense satisfactions of great food and wine, as well as the thrill of victories (Cubs win! Cubs win! Hey, hey!)—all of these point us toward ecstasies we will experience in the new Heavens and the new earth.

Life's pleasures—success at work, a good meal, a beautiful song, satisfying sex, a splendid aroma—are sacraments, yes sacraments, of the new Heavens and earth. Heaven is not designed for those who fear joy and pleasure and happiness, nor for those who deny such pleasures. Heaven is designed for those who relish pleasures and long for more.

HEAVEN IS UTOPIA

The book of Revelation's visions for the final Heaven are stacked with celebrations, music and songs, applause, festivals and festivities. In his study of how Jews at the time of the New Testament understood God's final utopia, Eric Gilchrest discovered the features of Jewish utopias. Jewish utopias involved wealth, the temple, rivers and water, wine and food, pleasant fragrances, music and light and great weather, peace, fellowship and society, plenty of work for each person, and the presence of God. Then he examined Revelation 21–22 and found nearly identical themes: the final Heaven, therefore, must be seen as a utopian vision.[6]

What is utopia? Full and lasting pleasure for all. With God at the center, we will be intoxicated with the deep, ecstatic joy of being known by God and knowing God. Plus, with God at the center, all pleasures will lead toward God, all happiness will be aimed at God, and all our pleasures will be attuned to God's pleasures.

Heaven is utopia, and a utopia can be described as our greatest deep joys on full display. We are leaning into that utopia of pleasure even now.

FROM ULTRASOUND TO AKSEL

Displayed on our microwave oven is a small, two-by-two-inch picture of a living human being in the womb of our daughter-in-law, Annika. The image is the ultrasound image of Aksel, our grandson. When we first saw this image, we stared at it, turned it, and moved it so we could take closer looks. We studied the picture so carefully that we thought we could identify (the as-yet unnamed) Aksel. He was a living human being, but he was nearly completely unknown to us. He was a gray image on a black background.

Then he was born. Suddenly, he became to us a living, colorful, crying, hungry, needy, and adorable little boy. Today we look forward to the times when he arrives at our house in his parent-driven car. Aksel unstraps himself from his child seat, opens the car door, and skips and hops and runs to the back door to let himself in. No sooner than he is through the door then off come his shoes, and he begins telling us a story about something that has happened.

Aksel knows that whatever he asks for, either Grandma or Grandpa will provide. Aksel is now a personality, known to us in his growth and development and what he likes (Minecraft) and what he doesn't like. In short, we knew his existence in the ultrasound, but we now know him face to face in living, interactive reality. The difference . . . well, knowing Aksel now is so amazing that we don't even look at the ultrasound image anymore. (And the same story can be told about our granddaughter, Finley, who is just as much a living personality of joy and love.)

Our pleasurable experience of God now is an ultrasound image compared to the living, interactive reality we will experience in Heaven. Our communing with God now, even in our best moments, is but a black-and-white, static image of the ecstatic union we will experience in Heaven.

I really must pause for a reminder. Heaven is God's promise that, on the basis of Jesus's bodily resurrection, we will be raised to a new kind of heavenly, embodied, ecstasy-seeking life. Once we make the resurrection of Jesus central to our view of Heaven, Heaven becomes a world of intense, ecstatic, embodied entirely holy pleasure and deep joy.

ALL THAT LOVE DESIRES AND EVERY CHAPTER BETTER THAN BEFORE

Jonathan Edwards was a theologian from the school of the ecstatic love for God. Edwards's theology presents the ultimate love of Father and Son and Spirit as what makes God what God is: love. When discussing what the saints will experience when they enter Heaven, Edwards said this: "They shall see in God every thing that gratifies love." That is as deep a sentence as you may ever read, and it may take years of reflecting on it daily to fully grasp what he means.

Edwards continued: "They shall see in him all that love desires. Love desires the love of the beloved. So the saints in glory shall see God's transcendent love to them; God will make ineffable manifestations of his love to them." Then the Puritan theologian takes us to the edge of human experience: "They shall see as much love in God towards them as they desire; they neither will nor can crave any more."[7]

In Heaven our desires will be perfected yet capable of ever more perfection. The perfected pleasure of Heaven will be to gaze on the face of God, to enjoy the beauty of our Father, and to dwell in the Spirit alongside our brother, the Lord Jesus, as we find our desires consumed by love of God and love of one another. "Love," Edwards stated, "desires union."

The final Heaven is all about the insatiable pleasure of that union.

Some think of Heaven in static terms—that is, endless sameness, good sameness, but still sameness. Others, and I'm sure they are right, understand Heaven to be full of growth and newness and surprises and development. Here we must cross over the line into a biblically informed imagination. In the last lines of *The Last Battle*, the last book in the Chronicles of Narnia, C. S. Lewis has Aslan reveal to the Pevensie children that there had been a railway accident and the family had died:

And as He spoke He no longer looked to them like a lion; but the things that began to happen after that were so great and beautiful that I cannot write them. And for us this is the end of all the stories, and we can most truly say that they all lived happily ever after. But for them it was only the beginning of the real story. All their life in this world and all their adventures in Narnia had only been the cover and the title page: now at last they were beginning Chapter One of the Great Story, which no one on earth has read: which goes on for ever: in which every chapter is better than the one before.[8]

In the summer of 2014, Kris and I were in Oxford where we took the tour of the university that focused on C. S. Lewis and J. R. R. Tolkien. We finished at Magdalene College, Lewis's college, where we walked around the grounds a bit. As we finished, our guide took us along the walk where Lewis was finally convinced there was a personal God who could be known. Our guide paused there, and from a small bag he pulled out a tattered copy of *The Last Battle*. Then as he fought back tears, he read aloud to us the last couple pages.

The prospect of pleasures evermore excites even the most familiar friend of C. S. Lewis.

The Fourth Promise:
Heaven Will Be Eternal Life

No human tears are beyond the
reach of God's infinite goodness.

— Jerry Walls

I am convinced we have not learned to read the Bible well enough to think about Heaven well.[1] Far too often we think of Heaven exclusively in individualistic terms: it is where *I* go when *I* die so *I* can be with God. Forever and ever. World without end. Amen.

I dare not diminish the importance of personal eternal life, but the Bible tells a story about Heaven that completes a narrative far bigger than that of personal salvation. The Bible's full story is the ultimate happy ending. All stories with a happy ending, one can rightfully say, are anticipations of Heaven's ultimate happy ending.

A few questions for you: What story do we need to know or see in the Bible so that the completion to the story is Heaven? What do the stories we love most tell us about our desire to participate in the new Heavens and the new earth? As we look at these questions and others, it will become clear that if we settle too easily into a cozy story where we find our souls nestled into the fullness of God's presence in private ecstasy, Heaven will come as a big surprise.

God designed Heaven for those who long for the completion to God's grand story, which does not begin or end with you or me.

A STORY IN SEARCH OF HEAVEN AS THE FINAL CHAPTER

The Bible tells a story that begins with God as the Creator who makes humans— that's us—in the image of God. It is right here where we often go wrong in our Bible reading, so we need to pause briefly to clarify just what it means to be made in God's image. It means God has created us and appointed us to represent God in the world, to mediate God to the rest of creation, and to govern and rule this world on God's behalf. We do these things as humans who love God and who love others. Out of that double-love, we learn how to govern as God governs.

Here is the mistake we are prone to make: we tip our hat to the concept of the image of God and rush on to the third chapter of Genesis—often referred to as the fall of Adam and Eve. It seems we are eager to make the observation that we are sinners. Then we learn to read the rest of the Bible as a story of *how to get personally saved from the Fall.*

Getting saved is important to the Bible, and getting saved personally is what getting into the final Heaven is all about. One world-religions author described each religion in a simple phrase. He summarized Christianity as the "story of salvation." So, yes, salvation is important. But the first two chapters of Genesis teach that we are God's images, and Genesis 3 tells us that we *failed in our image-bearing role of governing for God.* This simple observation leads to a profound shift in how to read the Bible: salvation in the Bible is a twofold act of God: a salvation *from* and a salvation *for.* We are saved *from* our sin and the world's systems, and this salvation heals, restores, and reconciles us with God so we can accomplish *our calling as image bearers.*

This makes all the difference for the subject at hand. If God's assignment for us is to be image bearers, then the final Heaven will be when we *live out that divine summons to be image bearers.* Which means Heaven is not an escape from this world but the *renewal of this world and our glorious opportunity to participate in and enjoy the created order as God designed it to be.* The Bible tells the story of salvation because we image bearers rebelled against God, and that rebellion released the contagions of disorder, chaos, sin, suffering, sickness, injustices upon injustices, and systemic evil. In fact, the last item just mentioned—systemic evil—is the reason for Heaven. Heaven, in order to *be what heaven is designed to be,* will undo systemic evil. As that happens, all rebellions will unravel—injustices, sicknesses, suffering, sin, chaos, and disorder. Heaven is when God releases the medicines that kill the contagions, when sin is eradicated, and when God's people will be what God wants them to be in the world. When the kingdom comes, sin will be no more.

In fact, on Heaven's gate will be a sign of memory: "No More!"

God designs heaven for those who long for the no-mores.

A SIGN ON HEAVEN'S GATE: NO MORE!

Please sit down with a Bible and read Revelation 20–22 a few times, without interruption. In your second reading jot down a list of everything that will be "no more" when God's kingdom is fully established. Here is my list:

No more . . .

- Death
- Hades
- Satan and his minions
- No more heaven (lowercase "h")
- Pain and tears
- Thirst and hunger
- Temple
- Sun and moon
- Night
- Impurity
- Evil
- Curse

These realities, some of which are simply limitations of life on earth while others are horrific experiences that deal death to us, will be no more. God will consign these things to history and they will be, like premodern medicine or Morse code or short shorts for basketball players, the No Mores of Heaven.

This list of No Mores contains even better news. We are meant to reverse those No Mores so that beyond each one is a positive. So,

- Instead of death, we will have endless, pulsating, *new creation life.*
- Instead of Hades, there will be *Heaven.*
- Instead of Satan and his minions, we will encounter *myriads and myriads of good angels.*

Heaven then is not just about the No Mores but also about the But This and Also That and Even More Look at This Too! If you were making a list of No Mores, what would you include? If you were to extend the list to add on the But Thises, what would they be? Go ahead, put this book or e-reading device down, grab a piece of paper, and write out in two columns what you think will be wiped from existence in Heaven and what will be in its place, throbbing with vitality in Heaven.

A famous Christian vision of Heaven from Ireland in the tenth and eleventh centuries is called *The Vision of Adamnan* (this could be called the Gaelic List of No Mores and But This). It closes with this beautiful balance of what will vanish and what will flourish.

No Mores

[Heaven will be] a kingdom without pride, or vanity, or falsehood, or outrage, or deceit, or pretence, or blushing, or shame, or reproach, or insult, or envy, or arrogance, or pestilence, or disease, or poverty, or nakedness, or death, or extinction, or hail, or snow, or wind, or rain, or din, or thunder, or darkness, or cold . . .

But This

a noble, admirable, ethereal realm, endowed with the wisdom, and radiance, and fragrance of a plenteous land, wherein is the enjoyment of every excellence.[2]

SOME NO MORES TO THINK ABOUT

Let's pause here to be reminded of the unthinkable. For millions of people the twentieth century was horror upon horror. Most students of government-inflicted deaths that occurred in this century, sometimes called *atrocitologists,* estimate that between *200 million and 240 million persons* died as a result of war, famine, persecution, and outright murder. Hitler's holocaust murdered some 6 million Jews, but we are talking about that number multiplied by thirty to forty. The total equals approximately two-thirds of America's population today. Roughly everyone living east of Denver represents those who were unjustly wiped from life during the last century. More than 200 million, and no one but God knows for sure how accurate those numbers are.

I recently read Miron Dolot's *Execution by Hunger,* a firsthand witness to the impact of Stalin's brutalities upon the farmers of Ukraine. They were forced into collectivization; their crops were stolen by the governments; their integrity and honor and histories were ripped up. Some 10 million Ukrainians were starved to death. Dolot's stories of pain, desperation, courage, and brutality strain belief and stagger the conscience.[3] What will Heaven mean for the victims of Ukraine's holocaust? The Heaven Promise is that all things—tragedies and holocausts—will be made right somehow.

Since *Roe v. Wade* was handed down in 1973, some 57 million babies have been aborted in the United States alone—six times the number of people who died in the Holocaust in Ukraine under Stalin. Since 1980 well over 1 billion babies have been aborted in the world. Twenty-one percent of all pregnancies in the United States end in abortion.[4] What, I ask myself, does Heaven mean for the innocent, millions and millions of children with entire lives stolen from them? In my own conscience, I stand in the tomb of Jesus and say, "The tomb is empty. Jesus is on the Throne. Jesus will make things right. God will create a Heaven where evil and injustices will be undone and rolled up into history."

At the great and final judgment, truth will be told, justice will be established, and the world will be put right—the world as God meant it to be. I imagine a Heaven flooded with little children who will grow into mature adulthood because

God will give them the chance to live as God intended for them to live. I know that *at least* that much will happen. And there could possibly be even more: their repentant mothers, reunited with aborted babies, could experience deep joy and be flooded with pleasure at seeing their little ones.

And as we all know, there is much more violence and death taking place. Every year more than five thousand women (and the numbers are assumed to be grossly underreported) are murdered on the basis of "honor killing" traditions. According to Amnesty International,

> Women are considered the property of male relatives and are seen to embody the honor of the men to whom they "belong." Women's bodies are considered the repositories of family honor. The concepts of male status and family status are of particular importance in communities where "honor" killings occur and where women are viewed as responsible for upholding a family's "honor." If a woman or girl is accused or suspected of engaging in behavior that could taint male and/or family status, she may face brutal retaliation from her relatives that often results in violent death. Even though such accusations are not based on factual or tangible evidence, any allegation of dishonor against a woman often suffices for family members to take matters into their own hands.

Amnesty International's final summons to the world is this:

> The murder of women in the name of "honor" is a gender-specific form of discrimination and violence. In societies where so-called honor killings are allowed to occur, governments are failing in their responsibility to protect and ensure women their human rights. "Honor" killings should be regarded as part of a larger spectrum of violence against women, as well as a serious human rights violation.[5]

While women are not the only victims of honor killings, they make up the vast majority. During the first hour of Heaven, these tragic injustices will be exposed for what they are, the perpetrators will confess their sins, the victims' voices will be heard, and God will make all things right.

The most important No More in Heaven is no more death, and in its place there will be Life for Evermore.

No More Death Because of Jesus's Resurrection and Gift of Life

A great misfortune of our society is that death is not a topic for discussion in polite company. We can't understand why families in the Middle East parade the casket of a lost loved one through a village in sorrow and mourning. The American strategy is to tame death into silence.

I was quite surprised recently when I grabbed a few well-known dictionaries of Christian theology from my shelf to look up what they said about death. Most of them had no entry or at best, a page or two. If theologians don't want to talk about death, who will? If the Christian faith isn't about undoing death, what is it? Our theologians are joining other Americans in silencing death, the latter by hiding death in a mortuary. We have learned to tame death with the phrases we use to describe it: *checked out, pushing up daisies, resting in peace, departed, exiting the stage, or taking a dirt nap.*

Even the practice of referring to death as the grim reaper reflects the language of defeat. In the Bible, death is a defeated enemy, not a stalking killer. God's aim is not to tame death or to silence death, but to defeat death by wrestling it to the ground, conquering the enemy, and finally slaying it. Death doesn't need to be tamed or managed or suppressed or run from or covered up in quiet rooms where folks mumble to one another. No, death needs to be killed and replaced with eternal life.

Approximately 600,000 Americans die each year from cancer and more than 7 million humans die of cancer worldwide each year.[6] This is why it's called the "emperor of all maladies." But in heaven, God will slay death and its creepy friend cancer. The multiplier of reckless cells will be sent back to the pit from where it originated, and death will be no more.

Ponder those you know who have died, stand in the empty tomb, and ponder now God's endless, creative life in the new Heavens and new earth.

The worst deal that death dishes out is that some die way too young.

THE STORY OF ZEKE HOLT

Zeke Holt's story has been told by his parents, Andy and Bree, who did their best to hold Zeke up as they stood for him in the empty tomb of Jesus. Shortly after the death of their four-year-old, Zeke, from Batten disease, Bree wrote on her blog:

> As most of you know, Zekey wasn't always showing his sickness. He was "healthy" all the way up to his 2nd birthday, where he walked, ran, communicated with a few words, laughed, showed sympathy for others, etc. All the things he was supposed to do, he did. Soon after, though, he lost his speech and the first major red flag was at 2.5 on May 18th, 2012 when he had his first seizure.
>
> Batten disease was a part of his make-up and we had no idea until that dreadful day, on July 30th, 2013, our hopes for his life to be returned to normal and freeing him from all that was taken from him through meds and extreme diet change . . . were crushed. . . .
>
> Saying goodbye to my Zekey, reading scripture to him, telling him over and over how much I loved him, how much of a blessing he was to me and to his daddy and siblings and all who knew him and of him. I told Zekey how much I felt honored to be his mommy and I meant it with my everything. It was the hardest thing I may ever have to do. I begged God to take him from this earth and back Home to Jesus, as Zekey's suffering became overbearing to see at the end. . . .
>
> I look forward to the day when I can hug a tall, handsome man—not calling him my son but my brother, telling him how proud I am of him and how honored I was to be his mother, even for a short 4 years, 4 months and 4 days. I will be on my deathbed, anxiously awaiting to see my Savior Jesus, my loving God and my so very strong Ezekiel Todd.[7]

His father, Andy, a pastor, said this on his blog:

Zeke is with Jesus. I'm jealous of them both.

I'm jealous of Zeke because he . . . gets to know Jesus face to face. . . .

I'm jealous of Jesus because he gets to talk to Zeke. Because of this
disease, I was never able to have a real conversation with him. . . . But now
that he's made whole, the first person he ever gets to converse with is Jesus. So
I'm jealous. . . .

For half of his life he suffered from the effects of seizures. Now, for
eternity, his body is made new, never to seize again.[8]

Weeks later Andy was asked how their family could possibly be doing so well,
and this is how he responded:

The only answer we have to that question is that we've found a hope that
transcends death. . . . This hope . . . is rooted in Jesus and his resurrection
from the dead.[9]

The reality of death, which the Holt family experienced tragically, is seen on
page after page in the Bible. Instead of silencing it or taming it, the Bible's authors
learned to embrace death and to defeat it with the glorious good news of the resurrection and new creation. Death may croak out its defiant words now, but in Heaven,
death's voice will be fatally silenced forever. The only voice allowed will be that of
life . . . for each of us in God's eternal global village.

The Fifth Promise: Heaven Will Be an Eternal Global Fellowship

> Simply seek happiness, and you are not likely to find it. Seek to create and love without regard to your happiness, and you will likely be happy much of the time. Seeking joy in and of itself will not bring it to you. Do the work of creating community, and you will obtain it—although never exactly according to your schedule. Joy is an uncapturable yet utterly predictable side effect of genuine community.
>
> — M. Scott Peck

Carl Linstrum had moved from the plains of Nebraska to the big city life of Chicago. Later, en route to Alaska from Chicago, he stopped off in Nebraska to visit friends. On that trip he encountered his childhood friend and now successful farmer, Alexandra Bergson.

With her sense of having accomplished so little in comparison to Carl, Alexandra expresses words of regret: "I'd rather have your freedom than my land."[1] She was comparing big-city freedom in small spaces with village space where everyone knows one another. Before we get to Carl's response, we'll ask this question: Will Heaven observe the big-city desire to be left alone, so-called freedom, or will it be more like small town neighborliness?

Now we come to Carl's response to Alexandra's desire for freedom, her yearning to break away from the tethers of community:

> Freedom so often means that one isn't needed anywhere. Here you are an individual, you have a background of your own, you would be missed. But off there in the cities there are thousands of rolling stones like me. We are all alike; we have no ties, we know nobody, we own nothing. When one of us dies, they scarcely know where to bury him. Our landlady and the delicatessen man are our mourners, and we leave nothing behind us but a frock-coat and a fiddle, or an easel, or a typewriter, or whatever tool we got our living by. All we have ever managed to do is to pay our rent, the exorbitant rent that one has to pay for a few square feet of space near the heart of things.

Carl's next words are some of the saddest lines in history:

> We have no house, no place, no people of our own. We live in the streets, in the parks, in the theatres. We sit in restaurants and concert halls and look about at the hundreds of our own kind and shudder.[2]

What is often taken to be freedom in the big city away from genuine community, as Willa Cather spells out in this brilliant dialogue in her novel *O Pioneers!*, is the loss of identity, the loss of family, the loss of place, the loss of village, the loss of fellowship, and the loss of a story that turns our life into final meaningfulness. Carl got his "freedom" from a traditional community, but he paid the price in the absence of village and friendships and, to be blunt, genuine love.

To answer our question, then: Heaven will be more like Alexandra's fellowship of village farmers than the dehumanizing anonymity Carl found in the city. Heaven will be a global village. Heaven is designed by God for those who want relationships with others in family and community. In the history of the church there have been three principal visions of what Heaven will be like: a kingdom, a city, and a garden.[3] Each of these images brings to the forefront an image of Heaven as a society. In the first, we have a king and we are citizens. In the second, we have dwellings and commerce and society and fellowship. And in the third, we are cultivators and producers and providers for our families. A single word that brings together kingdom, city, and garden is the word *village*.

God has promised us an eternal, global-village fellowship. To be ready for Heaven we will have to be raised into a new kind of embodied life, and the best example of what that life will be like is the resurrected body and life of Jesus. What happened after he rose from the dead? He immediately renewed fellowship with the apostles, he ate and drank with them, and he promised them abundance in the kingdom to come. Once we embrace the vision of Revelation 21–22 for the final Heaven, we know that the theocentric vision is just not enough. Instead, the final Heaven will be filled with loving relationships with other people in Heaven. God will be on his Throne, to be sure. But the final Heaven promises full fellowship for all people in it, forever.

Homes with Verandas

In entering into the village theme for the final Heaven, I am aware yet again of the need to remind ourselves that the Bible does not give us high-resolution pictures of Heaven. Rather, we have access to Heaven through impressions, images, and metaphors. I also am aware that our minds simply cannot comprehend all that God has prepared for those who love him.* But to whet our appetite, God has given to us images and impressions. One such image, straight from the lips of Jesus, is that he is preparing rooms in a home for us.† This image, of course, whets our appetite for Heaven as our final home.

What type of home do you think God has in store for us? Nigel Dixon, a leader of the church in Palmerston North (New Zealand), sketches the history of home architecture in New Zealand. Nigel shares an important discovery: prior to World War II, homes were built with verandas where you sat in the evening with your family and greeted passersby, some of whom found their way onto your veranda for fellowship. You would do the same as you walked past their home. But after the war,

---

* 1 Corinthians 2:9
† John 14:2–3

fewer homes were built with a veranda; in its place the back garden took priority. With this shift, people retreated from the rest of the world.[4]

In Heaven, I want to suggest our homes will have both a veranda for fellowship and a garden for retreat, a sacred place designed for fellowship and privacy. (Of course, I'm filling in an image—what matters most is fellowship and retreat, not the color of the ceiling on one's front porch. But sky blue is cool.) Nigel is right about city life today: "The public world knows no boundaries" today, and many are intent on carrying on their private life in public spaces. But Heaven will strike the perfect balance of privacy and devoted love of God, as well as fellowship and devoted love of family and others. We can't know this for sure, except to say this: we will love God, which means worship and adoration and communion with God; and we will love others, which means fellowship and sharing space, and we will do this in glorified but real bodies.

All this will be taking place in a community called the new Heavens and the new earth. What is fellowship like? Again, Nigel Dixon sums it up: membership, contribution and acceptance of the contributions of others, interdependence, and shared emotional connection. At least these (and surely much more and better) will be enjoyed in Heaven.

If our home in Heaven has a veranda, we might say TV life (as we know it) will disappear. Eccentric, insightful American writer David Foster Wallace, who comprehends what TV life means, shares his thoughts in one of the longest and still very readable sentences in American essays:

> If it's true that many Americans are lonely, and if it's true that many lonely people are prodigious TV-watchers, and it's true that lonely people find in a television's 2-D images relief from their stressful reluctance to be around real human beings, then it's also obvious that the more time spent at home alone watching TV, the less time spent in the world of real human beings, and that the less time spent in the real human world, the harder it becomes not to feel inadequate to the tasks involved in being a part of the world, thus fundamentally apart from it, alienated from it, solipsistic, lonely.[5]

Big city life versus the village, Carl versus Alexandra, lonely people watching TV versus loving people in relationship with others in the presence of God. Okay, maybe we will find the balanced joy of entertainment alongside fellowship with others, but I think you see the point.

Some of us think our neighbors ought to keep their distance for fear of overstepping boundaries between us. Others think we ought to be more neighborly, walking to and fro between homes. So let's get this straight: forget bad neighbors, remember your best neighbor, and now ramp that up a notch or two. Just when you have wrestled with yourself to the point where you will admit that there is such a thing as really good neighbors with whom you'd want not only to be neighbors but even to go on vacation with, now we are asking you to consider spending eternity with those same people. Sometimes on their veranda. If the great poet George Eliot can say, "In every parting [of friends] there is an image of death,"[6] we can answer back that in the resurrection all partings are stopped at the gate, all images of death are erased, and every parting leads to an eternal reunion.

KINGDOM BANQUETS

If we let the Bible shape our view of Heaven, we expect our schedules to be filled with banquets and feasts and parties. One of the first tasks for Jesus, once he snapped the bonds of death and returned to the land of the living, was to make what Eugene Peterson called "resurrection breakfast" for his friends.[7] In fact, Jesus invited seven of the apostles to the breakfast with these words: "Come and have breakfast."* Or as the King James Bible has it, "Come and dine." Either way, Jesus prepared for them an early-morning feast of tilapia they were likely never to forget.

Add John's vision to Jesus's resurrected reality: the first image of the kingdom of God in the final vision of Revelation† is a wedding's celebration of love and friendship and community. It's all about the banquet after the ceremony. (If a neighborly veranda in Heaven stretched your comfort zone, we're even now, since weddings

---

* John 21:12
† Revelation 21–22

make me a bit squirmy.) God has prepared the "Holy City, the new Jerusalem," and he lowers this bride-like city from the portals of the present heaven down to earth to create the eternal Heaven. The cosmic announcement is "Look! God's dwelling place is now among the people."* God among us in a brand-new, eternal city, which is expressed in the covenant language of a Jewish wedding. "They"—notice the plural (that is, all of us, God's worldwide family)—"will be his people, and God himself will be with them and be their God." One of the last paragraphs of the book of Revelation is the language of a wedding invitation: "The Spirit and the bride say, 'Come!'"† Heaven as a wedding banquet is a window, but it is a clear window: all of us, one big family, one big neighborhood, dwelling with God in the joyous fellowship we know at weddings.

Dining together with family and friends is one of life's greatest pleasures. Eugene Peterson has asked the right question to get us thinking about the prominence of banquets in the Bible's descriptions of Heaven: "Is there anything else we do as frequently and simply that combines necessity and pleasure so unselfconsciously, unpretentiously, and commonly as preparing and eating a meal with family or friends or guests?"[8] The answer is no several times over. Peterson is right about ordinary meals, but the Bible raises the meal a level or two. Kingdom meals seem to be banquets and feasts and parties and festivals. The most common image of meals in Heaven is a wedding feast, which was famous (just as they are today) for endless plans and preparation and, unlike today, an elaborate parade through town accompanied by musicians. Late in the evening, the decked-out bridegroom and friends would romp joyously and raucously through a village to the home of the bride. She was then escorted on a litter back to the groom's home. Of course, all of this was followed up with you-know-what, which then was followed by a weeklong party.[9] A wedding back then, just like today, meant a feast of cheesecakes and fruitcakes and dips and sauces and meats and grains and vegetables and fruits and olives and olive oil and of course the best wine the families could afford.

Heaven's banquets will be more diverse than those on Sesame Street and more

---

* Revelation 21:1–3
† Revelation 22:17

ethnic than Chicago's famous Taste of Chicago, because Heaven will be populated by all the tribes and nations of this world throughout all of history:

> The God who in ancient times called a specific ethnic people, the tribes of Israel, into a special relationship with himself has begun in these last days to establish a "holy race" made up of people from every tribe and tongue and nation. The God of Israel has addressed the Xhosa as "my people" and has called Polish laborers "the works of my hands." Mexicans have become "Abraham's off spring," and Koreans have been named "heirs according to the promise." The Lord has assembled together Scots and Swedes, Iranians and Navajos, and has addressed them, saying: "Once you were no-people, but now you are my people."[10]

Heaven will be what I have referred to as "a fellowship of differents."[11] All reconciled, all things forgiven, all back to loving relationships of trust and joy, and everyone will have a story to tell—one that all of us will want to hear. Heaven will be a global village where the verandas are filled with evening conversations among eternal neighbors.

A Village Where Everyone Is a Neighbor

Peter Kreeft has echoed a question that is heard repeatedly: "Will we recognize our friends in Heaven?" His answer is brilliant: "In fact, *only* in heaven will we really know our friends, from within."[12] I will supplement Kreeft with this: we will know one and all as friends. We will know people for who they are and for what they have done, the formerly ignored and invisible will be highly visible and impossible to ignore, and the anonymous will be famous figures impossible to overlook. The famed persons from this life also will be known, but no more known than anyone else. And always, God remains in the center. The lion of Judah and the Spirit dwell in the center. To capture this in one sentence does not do it justice, but here goes: Heaven will be all of us attending to God while knowing one another in an endless fellowship of deep joy.

I must tell you about the first African American woman to establish a four-year institution of higher learning. When I tell you her name below, it is not likely you will recognize it. But in Heaven she will be as famous as Beth Moore is today. She was the first African American woman to hold a high-level government directorship. She advised three American presidents and, between 1933 and 1945, according to one of her biographers, she was "arguably the most powerful African American person in the United States."[13]

Her parents were slaves; her mother's faith and piety were extraordinary and her father's faith was consistent. She grew up loved, and as a child she was given a New Testament to hold in church. But because she was black, education was not part of her childhood. Then the Presbyterian Board for Freedmen opened a school for children in Maysville, South Carolina, and she attended that school until she was about twelve, when she had to return to the cotton fields. Miracle of miracles, someone in far-off Denver sensed a whisper from God to give money to a child with potential, and our then-unknown woman was selected to attend Scotia Seminary in Concord, North Carolina. Her response? "I pulled my cotton sack off, got down on my knees, clasped my hands, and turned my eyes upward and thanked God for the chance that had come." Many neighbors saw her off to Scotia.

At Scotia, she entered a brick building for the first time, climbed stairs for the first time, and for the first time, had teachers who were African American. When she finished, she attended a school that later became Moody Bible Institute, where she experienced both a mighty baptism of the Holy Spirit and a calling to be a missionary to Africa. But the Presbyterians turned her down because they had no places for an African American female missionary.

So she went south and famously taught young African Americans; at one point, she had more than one thousand children in her Sunday school program. When she had the opportunity to move to Daytona Beach, Florida, to establish a college, she jumped on it. Her school was called the Daytona Educational and Industrial School for Negro Girls, where in 1904 her focus was evangelistic, educational, and geared toward social reform. When her school expanded into Bethune College, her curriculum was Bible, industry, and English. Today it is called Bethune-Cookman.

In 1936 she reflected on her life and her situation, as well as the way Christianity worked in the United States:

> The Negro must go to a separate church even though he claims to be of the same denomination as whites. He is not allowed to sing, in unison with the white man, the grand old hymns of Calvin, the Wesleys—the triumphant songs of Christ and eternal glory. When at last he is called to his final resting place on earth even his ashes are not allowed to mingle with those of his white brother, but are borne away to some remote place where the white man is not even reminded that this Negro ever lived. Judging from all that has preceded the Negro in death, it looks as if he has been prepared for a heaven, separate from the one to which the white man feels he alone is fit to inhabit.[14]

She experienced the utter violation of dignity that white folks used against African Americans, but that didn't stop her. She reversed the thunder of racism by conquering her enemies with love, with industry, with strategy, and with an educational system designed for the uplifting of women of all ethnicities but especially African Americans. We, and I say this bitterly, returned the favor by not even knowing her name.

Mary McLeod Bethune will be recognized in Heaven, and she will see—and maybe even more, white people will see—a Heaven not drawn into segregated churches, communities, and cemeteries. No, Heaven will be a fellowship of all races who will be given by God the dignity due each son and daughter.[15] When the cemeteries open their graves at the trumpet of the Lion of Judah, both communities and churches will experience new-creation community—and it will be a fellowship for all and including all.

Heaven will *at least* (while surely far more than this) be a reconciliation of all. Everyone will *at least* be neighbors and neighborly. Everyone, to borrow words from Martin Luther King Jr., will be "free at last" and will turn toward God in thanksgiving for their eternal freedom.

A Garden of Abundance

The Bible's descriptions of the new Heavens and the new earth are abundant with images of abundance. A good place to begin is by looking at Moses's grand pictures of abundance in the Promised Land. When God's people settle down with God, he promises:* "The Lord will grant you abundant prosperity"—in babies, livestock, and crops. One of my favorite expressions of blessing in the Bible is "You will be blessed when you come in [the house] and blessed when you go out." That covers it all, and this is just the entrée to the feast God is preparing. Jewish thinkers pondered this theme of abundance, and in the *Legends of the Hasidim,* two Jews get into a discussion:

> One says, "When the [Messiah] comes, everything will be wonderful. The Red Sea will be brandy."
>
> The other says, "Why not the Mediterranean? If you're going to believe in something, why believe in so little?"[16]

Brilliant. If Jesus can turn pots and pots of boring water into the best wine, why not have a Heaven symbolized by rivers and lakes and oceans of brandy. These images of wine and brandy are yet more symbols of relentless joy and celebration and fellowship and pleasure!

Think of how much God cared about the necessities of life in the daily supply of manna to his wilderness people,† a sign that God had his eye on the people to provide for them abundantly. But he did so only on a daily basis—so as to keep them from hoarding and to help them continue to trust God. When they arrived at their destination, God promised a "good land—a land with brooks, streams, and deep springs gushing out into the valleys and hills; a land with wheat and barley, vines and fig trees, pomegranates, olive oil and honey; a land where bread will not be scarce and you will lack nothing; a land where the rocks are iron and you can dig copper out of the hills."‡ Now we're talking.

---

* All from Deuteronomy 28, directly quoting verse 11, then verse 6.
† Exodus 16
‡ Deuteronomy 8:7–9

And what about this promise from Isaiah of what God will provide when God opens the storehouse of blessings for the people of God?

On this mountain the Lord Almighty will prepare
    a feast of rich food for all peoples,
a banquet of aged wine—
    the best of meats and the finest of wines.*

When Jesus turned water into the finest of Galilean wines at a wedding not far from his home, he anticipated just what Isaiah predicted: choice wine, the best meats, both in abundance, for God's people, in a colossal celebration.

Many of our celebratory meals, however, are cooked with a guilty conscience. We know there are people in poverty, people who are starving and will die from lack of nutrition. We know that people eat a handful of rice and drink dirty water each day, that parents weep at night because they can't buy food for their children, that people have barely enough. Meanwhile, we sit in comfortable homes with an abundance of food and wine and beer and juices. In Heaven there will be no hesitation. *Everyone will be at the table, and everyone will have his fill, and everyone will experience the bounty of God's provision.*

WHO IS ON YOUR
INVITATION LIST?

Let's think again about the image of eternal fellowship in an eternal global village. If this means we will find intense pleasure in loving others, and if everyone is a neighbor in Heaven, I have a question for you: *Who is on your dinner-invitation list?*

I long for the day when the Irish will be at peace with one another, when Germans will be at peace, when Serbians and Slavs will be at peace, when Israelis and Palestinians will sit down for dinner, when Afrikaners and Africans will put aside their grievances, and when America's northerners and southerners will drop their

---

* Isaiah 25:6

stereotypes, when America's African Americans and Latin Americans and Asian Americans and European Americans see themselves as one.

Assuming you have some convictions about who will be there, who is on your invitation list? Who will you welcome to your veranda for late-morning coffee? Adam and Eve, Abraham and Sarah, David, Solomon, Isaiah, Jeremiah, Ezekiel, Peter, Paul, John, Mary, Junia, Phoebe, Priscilla, Huldah, Miriam? Or will it be Justin Martyr, Perpetua, Macrina, Augustine and his mom, St. Thomas, Luther, Calvin, Jonathan Edwards, Sarah Osborn, Wesley and his mom. Or maybe Rebecca Protten, Henrietta Mears, Beth Moore, Martin Luther King Jr., Nelson Mandela, Archbishop Desmond Tutu. Or perhaps George Whitefield, Charles Finney, D. L. Moody? I will first invite Dietrich Bonhoeffer, and I hope he says, "Herr McKnight, *jawohl, ich bin schon bereit.*"*

---

* Mr. McKnight, yes, I'm already ready.

The Sixth Promise: Heaven Will Be an Eternal Beloved Community

> Among all things, however disparate, there reigns an order, and this gives the form that makes the universe resemble God.
>
> — Dante Alighieri

> The kingdoms of our world, including many religious kingdoms, run on doctrinal fear the way the kingdom of God runs on grace.
>
> — Dallas Willard and Gary Black Jr.

Heaven can't get going until evil is done away with, until sin is erased, and until all injustices are locked into history's past. God has promised this in the Heaven Promise. As Rich Mouw once described it, Heaven begins when "[God] will destroy all of those rebellious projects that glorify oppression, exploitation, and the accumulation of possessions." He was speaking of a Heaven without violent powers—physical, social, and economic. In other words, "a political reckoning must occur, and the power that has been misused in political history must be handed back to its proper source."[1] There will be no injustices, or as Peter Kreeft said, in a nuanced way, no more "unjust *distributions* of pleasures and pains, opportunities and rewards on earth."[2]

God designed Heaven for those who long for God's beloved community. This story has a perfect ending. It begins with the story of God's creation of humans as his special image bearers. Then comes the nasty day that established human rebellion, followed by the formation of God's people, which led to the sending of the Messiah to rule those people. That story longs for the day when God's people live in God's way in God's renewed creation. That is the story of the new Heavens and the new earth.

The Bible looks for a just society, and most people who hope for Heaven are longing for justice, but far too many talk about Heaven as if it will be a private country club. We need to do some serious private pondering about what God wants and what we want. If we return to the two big theories about Heaven, far too many people want *only* a theocentric heaven and have little concern for a kingdom-centric heaven. So it seems to me that when the gates into the New Jerusalem fly open there will be a learning curve for many: we will all see that God designed Heaven to be a space where everyone will be flooded with love for God *and* love for one another.

Injustice will be chased away. Perhaps the Bible's best example (other than perhaps the beautiful attempts in ancient Israel in its legislation) is found in Acts 2:42–47. That is when the Spirit of God filled the formerly unjust spaces of economic and social exploitation with God's beloved community. What did that look like?

> All the believers were together and had everything in common. They sold property and possessions to give to anyone who had need. Every day they continued to meet together in the temple courts. They broke bread in their homes and ate together with glad and sincere hearts, praising God and enjoying the favor of all the people.

And the apostle Paul spoke of a new kind of community when he said the Corinthians needed to learn the principles of mutual reciprocity:[*]

> Our desire is not that others might be relieved while you are hard pressed, but that there might be equality. At the present time your plenty will supply what

---

[*] 2 Corinthians 8:13–14

they need, so that in turn their plenty will supply what you need. The goal is equality.

But Paul took a bold step that often is missed. To the masters in Colossae, and I mean those who in the Roman system had slaves, Paul says,* Masters, provide your slaves with what is right and *equal.*

Many translations use the word *fair,* but Paul's word is stronger than that. His word refers to the distribution of material goods among those who live faithfully under King Jesus. They were to share with one another so that each would have what each needed.

Heaven is designed so that *each person will have what each person needs, and so that each community will have what each community needs.* The world's system, shaped as it is by the Beast of Revelation, does not care about provision for all. Instead, the Beast far too often pursues materialistic indulgence by exploiting the weak and poor, or the Beast unjustly takes from those who have to give to those who have not earned it or who already have too much. But in Heaven the Beast will be no more.

SATIRES ABOUT THE BEAST

In the book of Revelation, John keeps his eyes on the Beast of Babylon, the symbol he uses to portray violence, rebellion against God, and the one who is the architect of systemic injustice. John is of course talking about the Roman empire and its brutal emperors who, instead of love, doled out abusive power; instead of justice, created hierarchical prejudice and bias; instead of wisdom, established control; instead of respect, permeated the empire with status assignments; instead of food, gave the poor what was left over while the rich ate and dwelled in opulence—on the backs of the poor.

There is a famous satirical novel from the first century about the Roman love for feasting by Petronius, a well-known "judge of eloquence," called *The Satyricon.*

---

* Colossians 4:1; the KJV and WEB translations have "equal" while most have "fair."

Revelers arrive at Trimalchio's home* for a feast after they had been to public baths for a massage. But as they enter, they observe a sign threatening one hundred stripes for any slave who leaves the home. In the entry, they see a magpie in a golden cage and a long wall painting celebrating (heroically) the life of Trimalchio. Orders were barked out when they entered the dining room: they were to step first with the right foot.

They sat down and began singing. Meanwhile, "boys from Alexandria poured water cooled with snow over our hands" while others pared their hangnails. A dish had a side of white and black olives, small mice (yes, that's right) rolled in honey and poppy seeds, along with hot sausages with plums and pomegranate seeds. Then enters Trimalchio himself, propped on "a nest of small cushions" and dressed up in what we would call bling-bling.

The dinner goes on and on with provisions of wine with which to wash one's hands and then abundances of all sorts of meats and vegetables and grains and fruits and wine—with the announcement *Vinum vita est* ("wine is life")—and dancers and drunkenness and vomiting and urinating and servants rushing here and there and vulgar behaviors and music and girls and boys available for sexual favors. This satire, written by Petronius, does what Revelation does: it satirizes indulgence, opulence, and exploitation.[3] Only the Bible goes further! Instead of poking fun at the revelries of the rich and famous, the Bible points the reader to the final judgment of God.

Good satire exaggerates reality. We encounter a more noble satire in the eighteenth chapter of Revelation, where we read a description of the Beast of Babylon. The Beast created a powerful, successful empire shaped through and through by violence, bloodshed, murder, and injustices. It all was done on the back of the poor who made Rome, well, Rome. I urge you to read a sampling of these words carefully to see how confrontational they are. What you will see is a satire on the injustices of Rome, and as you read, imagine you are a first-century Christian, suffering under Rome's oppression and hearing these words as if for the first time. If you put yourself in his place, you will hear John's original message: *God's judgment is coming*

---

* Some think Trimalchio represented the insatiable appetite of the emperor Nero. Petronius joined Nero in his revelries.

*against injustices of all sorts, God will save his people, and in God's heavenly, be-
loved community economic and material justice will permeate every fabric of
society.**

Perhaps we need a reminder: John has his eyes fixed on Rome and his finger
pointed at the emperor. His concerns are rebellion against God, exploitation of the
poor, and indulgence in every form of sin. He announces God's judgment on all
injustices:

> "Fallen! Fallen is Babylon [Rome] the Great!"
>> She has become a dwelling for demons
> and a haunt for every impure spirit,
>> a haunt for every unclean bird,
>> a haunt for every unclean and detestable animal.

He points at Rome's essential sin: arrogance.

> In her heart she boasts,
>> "I sit enthroned as queen.
> I am not a widow;
>> I will never mourn."

He reveals that Rome's friends of opulence will turn against Rome:

> When the kings of the earth who committed adultery with her and shared
> her luxury see the smoke of her burning, they will weep and mourn over her.
> Terrified at her torment, they will stand far off and cry:

> Woe! Woe to you, great city,
>> you mighty city of Babylon!
> In one hour your doom has come!

---

* Revelation 18

Now John beckons the cosmos to rejoice over God's just judgment of Rome and its ways:

> Rejoice over her, you heavens!
>> Rejoice, you people of God!
>> Rejoice, apostles and prophets!
> For God has judged her
>> with the judgment she imposed on you.

Perhaps this bold satire of Rome seems irrelevant because you want to know more about Heaven. Yet we *must* see the central significance of this vision of Rome's downfall in order to understand what Heaven is all about. Here is our shared problem: our view of Heaven is too small. We think in terms of going to be with God when we die; we think of our own personal eternal life with God. Now we may add to that our joy that others we know will also be with God. But the Heaven Promise is far grander and greater than our own eternity. God promises an eternal, beloved community. For that community to be established, the walls of this world's exploiting powers must come down, the streets of the exploiting opulent must be rerouted, and the sinful patterns of the exploiting authorities eradicated. The exploited will be lifted up in the kingdom of God.

If in Heaven God will fully and finally establish justice on every corner, in every shop, and in each home, he can do so *only by removing injustice*. The great news for most people—from those suffering in Africa to those held in the sex slavery of India to the sweatshops of China to the racism of the United States and to worldwide oppression of women—is ending injustice and bringing justice are the deepest hope that leads the oppressed to the prayer, "Come, Lord Jesus."

FROM BABYLON TO THE NEW JERUSALEM

Something happens in the book of Revelation that cannot be missed: the wealth and power of Babylon will be packed up, put on boats, and shipped to the New Jerusalem *where those same goods and foods will be directed toward devotion to God and the*

Lamb! The new Heavens and the new earth are described by John as abundant wealth:* filled with sparkling jewels, impressive architecture measured with a rod made of gold, walls of jasper, the city of pure gold and precious stones, twelve gates made of twelve pearls, and streets of gold. The inhabitants of the New Jerusalem will have all the food they need (and more), all the wine they want (and more), all the fragrances and colors and art they've ever enjoyed (and more), all the work they've ever desired (and more), and all this in a city of splendid weather. High and lifted up in the middle of this city will be God—the Father, the Son, and the Spirit—to the praise of all creation.

The story must be told: what was gained unlawfully and the excesses of exploitation will be returned to their proper Owner, the Lord over all lords, as a gigantic thanksgiving offering, a display of devotion, and as provision for God's beloved community.

Call it what you want—the Eternal Reversal or the Endless Jubilee or even the Return to the One True Owner—but what we read in Revelation is that exploitation will end, a just economy will become the only norm, and all of it will be an offering to the God of Heaven.

Two points: first, we live in the Babylon of injustice now but, second, Babylon will someday be defeated.

A Garden, Abundance, Food and Business Deserts

One day I was lecturing at Northern Seminary on the apostle Paul's vision of a church in which all boundaries were broken down by fellowship in Christ. There would be, as Paul put it, neither Jew nor Greek, slave nor free, male nor female.† I used the image of a salad bowl because, like a salad, the church is designed to be a mixture of different sorts of vegetables and fruits and nuts and cheese (that is, race, economic status, and gender). When the class was over, an African American student, a pastor in Chicago, asked if he could say something privately. In the hall he said, "I love your salad bowl story. It works for me. But I want you to know that in my community no one eats a salad because there are no grocery stores." He

---

* Revelation 21
† Galatians 3:28

introduced me to the reality of "food deserts," where the Beast has taken hold of the provisions. In modern-day Babylon, conditions of injustice, exploitation, and lack of healthy provisions lead to this:

No grocery stores.

In America.

The children who suffer the most are not to blame.

Systemic evil settles in and creates Babylons.

Injustices run wild.

And it's much worse in other parts of the world.

Jennifer Wehunt in *Chicago Magazine* described the food-desert realities so many in our country experience day to day, month to month, year to year:

> In the northeast corner of 101st Street and Princeton Avenue, a peeling sign lists activities forbidden by the 100th South Princeton Block Club: loitering, drug dealing, loud music. When Edith Howard moved from the projects to this block of brick bungalows in 1964, the neighborhood—Roseland— seemed a promising place to give her growing family a better life. But the Roseland of today is much changed: The block club hasn't been active for years, and drug and gang activity is common. What's more, Roseland lacks many of the basic resources that stabilize a neighborhood, including a good place to buy food. For groceries, Howard, 78, relies on her daughter to drive her the two and a half miles up to Chatham or down to the border of Morgan Park. . . .
>
> Howard is one of the 609,034 Chicagoans who live in what's known as a food desert, a concentrated area short on access to fresh meat and produce, but flush with the packaged and fried yield of convenience stores and fast-food outlets.[4]

Food and business deserts are created by the Beast.[*] Heaven will strip the Beast of power, and in Heaven grocery stores with fresh vegetables and fruits will gladly

---

[*] Our economic life is not simple and humans are responsible in the injustices of food deserts, but the Beast desires to work in human responsibility and irresponsibility to create systemic evil.

and generously serve every neighborhood. The student who reminded me that he and his family and his neighbors could not buy salad at a neighborhood store added, "Someday, I believe, there'll be a grocery store in my neighborhood. Then we'll eat salads, but not now, at least not very often." We can be inspired to replenish the food deserts of our cities on the basis of the Heaven Promise.

His Name Is Stanley Ratliff

Injustices run wild in Babylon, and Babylon is closer than you may know.

He sat in my class at Northern Seminary rarely speaking a word. But another student in class, Phil, once said, "You need to ask Stanley about his story." So I did, and Stanley eventually gave me a book that told his story. It's called *A Dream, A Goal, Never a Reality: A True Story of Superior Movement.* Stanley is an African American, from Chicago's West Side, and he was a lead singer in a band called Superior Movement. Think Motown, think matching suits on five dancing black men wearing Afros, singing and turning nightclubs into night rhythms. Think inexperienced, think taken advantage of, think hard work and constant temptation. Think constant gigs and a tour that took the group to New York City. Think drinking rum and cola daily and think cocaine and free-basing.

Stanley ran into an old friend, Donnie, who came to Stanley's home for a birthday party. Stanley confessed sinister workings underfoot: "All of my life I had never hung out with anyone selling drugs. . . . [Donnie] was a good-hearted person, but when he realized the police were setting him up, he put me into the picture." On his way home from driving students in the local school's van, Stanley saw Donnie's van, so he stopped to see if Donnie was in it. Donnie came out and gave Stanley the keys to his (Donnie's) van and asked Stanley to drive. And so Stanley was set up. Shortly thereafter, the police surrounded the car and Stanley was arrested for dealing drugs.

I have to say that a black man on trial, even with Donnie's letter saying Stanley was framed, can lead to yet another sad display of injustice in America.

Stanley got out on bail and started attending services at Lawndale Community Church. He went to church with enthusiasm and began attending a Bible study as well. Every week he went to church, while the case continued for eight months. It seemed hopeful, since Donnie had given testimony to the judge that Stanley had been set up. But when verdict time came, Stanley was found guilty and sent to prison. What happened is the all-too-common reality for many African American males.[5]

In his book, Stanley wrote:

> All the undercover agent had to do was tell the truth.
>
> But such is the case with many young black boys who don't have the right of [or funds for good] representation when they go to court. They get railroaded into a corrupted judicial system and then are assigned a number for the rest of their life.[6]

The jury had been racially imbalanced. The state's attorney had accused him of being a drug dealer. Four hours after the verdict, my friend and student, Stanley Ratliff, was on his way to prison.

His current pastor and my colleague at Northern Seminary, Wayne Gordon, pastor of Lawndale Community Church, finishes Stanley's story in his own book:

> I [Wayne] wept uncontrollably right there in the courtroom as they took Stanley away to prison. . . . Every Friday, Stanley called me collect from prison. . . . Every few months I made the hundred-mile trip to visit him in Dixon. . . . So the church adopted [Stanley's girlfriend] Antoinette and her two boys . . . and moved them into one of the apartments we [the church] owned.[7]

When the judge decided he would hear a plea for clemency, Wayne and others from Lawndale went to the hearing to speak on Stanley's behalf in December 1991:

> I [Wayne] delivered what I think was the most moving and persuasive sermon I have ever preached.

In February 1992 the governor pardoned Stanley for a crime he had not committed. Antoinette asked Wayne to go to the prison and bring Stanley back home, which he did.

On our way back home, Stanley and I spent most of the time shouting, singing, and praising God. As we arrived at Stanley's home we saw a crowd of people had gathered. . . . Antoinette stood there, holding Stanley's baby son, whom he had never seen. . . .

I asked Stanley about what it was like in prison. "You know, Coach," he said, "it wasn't that bad." While in prison Stanley had completed his college degree. He had led the music every week at Bible study and for the Sunday service. He had read through the Bible at least twice and had regularly shared his faith with others. . . .

Two weeks after he was released, we had the wedding during Sunday morning worship. . . .

Today there is a tremendous man of God at Lawndale Community Church who serves the church full-time as an assistant pastor in charge of our worship and music. He also has an outreach ministry to men in prison, and he works with JoJo at Hope House, ministering to men recently released from prison.[8]

Stanley is a sweet-spirited man who knows injustice, but he is now flourishing in a ministry to the formerly incarcerated. Stanley has tasted a little bit of hell and a little bit of heaven, and he knows that beyond the grave justice will flow like a river. He'll get those two years back, *at least.*

Heaven will be a place where no injustices occur and where all injustices of the past will be set right. Is our view of Heaven big enough to enable us to long for—to inspire us to long for the days when there will be no more injustice? When the New Jerusalem will flow with justice for all, young and old, for all races, for both genders, and for all people—from the poorest to the richest who will share in God's bounty? The Heaven of the Bible is all about God's beloved community watered by the river of God's grace and justice and peace.

We are now finished looking at God's six promises about Heaven. Before we move to the top-ten questions about Heaven, we need to look at two more ideas:

1. What the first hour in Heaven will be like if these six promises are true.

2. How Heaven people ought to live now.

The First Hour in Heaven

The Promise of Reconciliation

You can't out-sin God's grace. Period.

— David Swanson

I do not know exactly when this will happen, but it will happen before anything else happens. It has to.

Heaven is permeated with grace and love and peace and reconciliation. In Heaven all things will be made right. I refer to the "first hour" in Heaven because that is when we all will suddenly, fully, and eternally realize the many-directional fullness of God's promise.

Here is my claim:

The first thing that will happen in Heaven, on the road up to the gates or at the gate or just inside the gates, is this: we will face God and one another and be fully reconciled.

Rich Mouw has asked the right question:

Will there not be a very special and profound sadness that falls over the [heavenly] City when the accounts must finally be settled between the Catholics and the Protestants of Ireland, between Mennonite martyrs and their Calvinist [and Lutheran] persecutors, between Christian plantation owners and their Christian slaves?[1]

If Heaven is where everyone loves everyone well, then reconciliations are to be expected. You can't love if you are at war with one another. So the first thing that happens in Heaven is you will be face to face with everyone with whom you are at odds, and with everyone with whom you are in complete peace. We don't know if this will happen instantaneously, so that we will barely recognize it, or if this will happen in a powerful revelation in our deepest consciousness. Or perhaps it will be a little more like how reconciliation occurs right now (when it happens). But it will happen. Or it won't be Heaven. Heaven is where and when all things are made right.

Reconciling with all others is important, in part because it contradicts the theocentric theory of Heaven. For many people Heaven is little more than personal, private, individual union with God with scarcely any attention (or none) paid to others. Heaven for these people is imagined as being all about God and the individual—just the two of us. But, as we have taken pains to emphasize, the final Heaven of the new Heavens and the new earth is profoundly social—a grand fellowship of a grand family. To use earlier terms: Heaven will be both theocentric and kingdom-centric. The moment we embrace Heaven as the utopian society of love and peace and justice, we also embrace that we will embrace not only God but also one another.

For that kind of embracing reconciliation to occur, there has to be honesty, vulnerability, and authenticity. You have to be the real you, and I, Scot, have to be the real Scot. Which means we will be face to face with our enemies and those with whom relationships are anything but warm. Face-to-face meetings will lead to deep truth telling, confession, and admission. There will be no hiding and pretending or softening or reframing in an attempt to look better than we are.

FACE TO FACE WITH ALL FOR ALL ETERNITY

Face-to-face meetings, truth telling, repentance, embraces, and reconciliation. These are the themes of the first hour in Heaven, and no one is more awakened of late to this theme than Dr. Leslie Leyland Fields. Once while she was praying and meditating over the Lord's Prayer, Leslie mused, *"Does 'Honor your father' apply to us,"* I questioned, *"those of us who have been hurt and deceived and abandoned by our mothers or fathers, or even both? . . .* Neither did I care to forgive my father and all that had been done in the rooms and houses of my childhood where he sometimes sat and walked—and walked away from." She puts her pain into another question: "What could be more unnatural, more upside down, than this: the ones who bring us into the world abandoning us to the world?" Leslie and her siblings stole food and clothing; they kept a tight guard around the harsh truth about their home life; they descended into a life of shame and barely knew it. When Leslie wrote her first book, she sent her father a copy—to which he never responded.

Let's fast-forward to the first hour in Heaven. We have a father who probably had schizoid personality disorder and whom Leslie once described as a "sad, pathetic lump of a man whose only achievement was siring six human beings, one of whom he molested, all of whom he seemed to disavow."

Leslie's sister Laurie once informed Leslie that "Dad used to come into my room." Leslie asked, "What? What do you mean? How often?" Laurie then said, "Whenever he could. For many years. That's why I would run away at night."

Leslie's question haunts but not as much as does her sister's response: "Laurie, why didn't you tell me?"

"What could you have done, Leslie? There was nothing you could have done." She closes with "Dad ruined my life, you know?"

Leslie and Laurie have done their best to forgive their father. Let us suppose the unfathomable, that on the far side of death at the gate of Heaven, they will be face to face with their father. That's the moment when truth will fall from the skies with lightning flashes of eternal horror revealing the sinfulness of it all. But the shout of horror somehow will have an echo of thunder that is all grace. Both horror and grace simultaneously.

In that first hour. "Forgiveness," Leslie knows, "requires remembrance. We cannot confess and name what was done without memory."[2]

There will come a moment when the perpetrator fully realizes what he has done and fully embraces his sin. The victims will find full vindication and justice and truth and grace and embrace. Not until then can the thunderous echo of eternal joy be heard in Heaven. When we pass through that moment, the brass and strings and percussion and voices all will lift their voices to the praise of God's glorious, transforming grace. I can't imagine the first hour without someone belting out "Amazing Grace"! Leslie and Laurie will be in the front row of the choir.

Every sin we have committed, every evil system we have created, every moment we have rebelled against the goodness of God will be made right. We will be made right, and we will make things right with others.

Truth must be settled in the first hour, and people must be reconciled. If there are tears in Heaven, they will occur in the first minutes of the first hour. If there are no tears in Heaven, it is because truth-telling-based repentance will be instantaneously swallowed up in the deepest kind of reconciliation. We will embrace each other in the kind of love God alone knows—the eternal interlocking dance of the Father, Son, and Spirit. We will lock arms and slap one another's backs, and we will say, "Come on over for coffee, you and your family! We'll have a party and celebrate the grace of forgiveness and love and reconciliation."

For some this is so frightening that they may want to avoid thinking about it. I understand that, but we have to back up to see two eternal, unstoppable truths:

First, God is reconciled within the Trinity: Father and Son and Spirit love
and adore one another in an endless dance of joyous communion.

Second, God will be reconciled with us, and that means with each of us.

Because of the permeating influence of God's powerful grace of truth, repentance, forgiveness, embrace, and reconciliation, we too will be reconciled with others. The reconciled God will fill us with reconciliation graces and powers. Tutsis will sit down with Hutus, Germans will sit down with Russians, Russians with Ukrainians, and southerners will sit down with northerners in America. And it gets even more personal. Unfaithful-but-redeemed husbands will sit down with destroyed-but-healed wives, fathers will sit down with broken-but-new-creation children, neighbors will sit with neighbors, workers with workers . . . The gate will be filled with renewed, restored, and refreshed relationships so that the glory of God's grace and new-creation power are the only songs sung for ages.

You and your mom, you and your dad, you and your siblings, you and your friends, you and your spouse, you and your children, you and your in-laws and grandchildren, all will be encircled in a grand embrace of grace and forgiveness and repentance and restoration and reconciliation.

Kris and I have a buoyant friend, Katie, a lovely young woman who was the driver of a car that flipped over, resulting in the death of her college-age friend. That event changed our friend's life forever. The father of the young woman who died sent Katie the message "I love you" the night of the accident, and when they met at the funeral, he embraced her and repeated his words. Maybe the hardest words a father could have said were maybe the most important words Katie has ever heard. His words still comfort Katie when the memories of the accident awaken her in the deepest sort of sorrow. But these three—father, deceased daughter, and Katie—all will enter into the first hour of Heaven. Now I imagine: Before that first hour occurs, our friend Katie will walk up the path to the New Jerusalem and there, waiting at the gate, will be her friend with her arms opened wide. I imagine her friend's words will be, "Katie, we've been waiting for you. What took you so long?!"

After reading this paragraph about herself, Katie, a lover of books, sent me one of her favorite lines about Heaven from a mutually appreciated author. Marilynne Robinson once put into the mouth of Pastor John Ames this belief about Heaven: "In eternity this world will be Troy, I believe, and all that has passed here will be the epic of the universe, the ballad they sing in the streets."[3] When I read that line recently in re-reading *Gilead*, I thought of Katie and what memory of that epic of the universe now means and what it will mean then. What it will mean is that the epic will be transformed into an even greater story.

Whenever these embraces occur—at the moment of death, in the searching lights of God's judgment, or in Heaven—what I am calling the first hour in Heaven will occur because it is final and full reconciliation that will make Heaven heavenly.

In Heaven We Will Remember

In Heaven we will remember our lives and comprehend them beyond what we now can remember. Our memories will be healed because they will be swallowed by the kingdom story that makes sense of all things. Miroslav Volf, one of America's finest theologians, endured searching interrogations by Captain G during his military service for Yugoslavia. The point of inquiry was Volf's Christian faith. And he knew what his memories of Captain G could do to him if he allowed them to fester. He has written of the piercing significance of what memory does to us: "My soul was at stake in the way I remembered Captain G."[4]

We all know that we can remember in a way that remakes a painful memory into a sword that is used against others and even ourselves. So long as our memory is a sword, we are not healed. So Volf, having learned to process the violence he suffered, encourages us to learn to remember the way the Exodus and the Passion are memorialized. Both the slavery behind the Exodus and the suffering at work in the Cross were swallowed up into a grander story of grace—entrance into the Promised Land and resurrection into the presence of God.[5] Slavery and crucifixion became elements in the stories of liberation and resurrection. When you see slavery as creating a story of liberation, slavery is diminished; when you see the crucifixion in light of the empty tomb, the crucifixion's pain is transformed.

If memory shapes our identity, then in Heaven we will not forget. Some would say we will have even keener memories in Heaven. But will we remember our pains and sufferings? What Volf has shared leads us to say that we will remember the violence of our own stories in the context of what God has made of them in the kingdom of God. We will remember our suffering the way the elderly remember a broken ankle suffered many years ago, the way we remember the loss of a long-ago job and how it opened doors to a more expansive career, the way we remember a love lost when the love we found later was even better.

Notice how memory, from Heaven's angle, plays out. In Jesus's parable about the rich man and Lazarus, each remembers life on earth. The martyrs in God's presence remember their sufferings. At the judgment in the first hour of Heaven, we will give an account of what we have done in the body, and to do that we must have our memories still intact.* Yes, we will remember. But what we remember will be seen for the role it played in God's grand story of love and justice and peace and pleasured joy in Heaven.

"To Stand in Your Line"

From the first hour on, we will understand everything that ever happened to us, everyone we knew. Every moment of every day, week, month, and year will suddenly make sense. And we will continue to explore our past as we enter more deeply into the story of God in Heaven's exploration of the lands beyond the future.

In Mitch Albom's mega-best-selling novel *The Five People You Meet in Heaven,* the dramatic teaching moment comes when his character, Eddie, who has just died, enters into paradise and is instructed on the mission of Heaven itself. It is a brief episode worth telling because, fiction or not, Albom points us to what Heaven will be for all of us, a time when the whole of our lives will suddenly make sense:

> "There are five people you meet in heaven," the Blue Man suddenly said.
> "Each of us was in your life for a reason. You may not have known the reason at the time, and that is what heaven is for. For understanding your life on earth."
> Eddie looked confused.
> "People think of heaven as a paradise garden, a place where they can float on clouds and laze in rivers and mountains. But scenery without solace is meaningless.
> "This is the greatest gift God can give you: to understand what happened in your life. To have it explained. It is the peace you have been searching for."
> Eddie coughed, trying to bring up his voice. He was tired of being silent.
> "I am your first person, Edward. When I died, my life was illumined by five others, and then I came here to wait for you, to stand in your line, to tell

---

* Luke 16:25; Revelation 6:9–11; 2 Corinthians 5:10. My thanks to Tara Beth Leach for comments on the importance of memory in Heaven.

you my story, which becomes part of yours. There will be others for you, too. Some you know, maybe some you didn't. But they all crossed your path before they died. And they altered it forever."6

The first face-to-face encounter will be with God, who will make sense of all our stories. It is not fanciful, so it seems to me, to imagine standing in line to pass the peace and grace of our life on to others, and it is even less hard to imagine this going on eternally with all the inhabitants of Heaven, not just five.

So, What Happens First?

To dwell in God's Heaven we must be reconciled with God, with ourselves, and with everyone else. To be reconciled we have to forgive and be forgiven. In the first hour, by an act of God, we will all be reconciled to love one another forever. I believe we will be fully conscious and fully cooperative in this grand and glorious moment.

How Should Heaven People
Live Today?

The Challenge to Be Heaven People on Earth

Heaven intrigues, consoles, and inspires.

—Alister McGrath

How can we live if we are going to die, and
how can we die if we are going to live forever?

—Graham Twelftree

Sometimes it seems there are two sides cheering in the gym. One group yells out, "More heaven!" and fans of that team repeat the cheer. The other group yells, "More life now!" and like-minded fans declare the same.

Gary Scott Smith, in his book *Heaven in the American Imagination*, sides more with the first group. He wrote, "If an afterlife exists, worldliness is escapism."[1] I heard a preference for escapism in my childhood Christianity whenever we sang Jim Reeves's famous song, "This world is not my home / I'm just a-passing through."[2]

The other side has its own notable list of fans, including the late, well-known liberal theologian-pastor of Manhattan's Riverside Church, Harry Emerson Fosdick. He once said, "Our mission is not to get men to heaven" but "to bring heaven to earth."[3] Standing alongside Fosdick is Charles Reynolds Brown, former Dean at Yale Divinity School, who dressed up Fosdick's statement with concrete realities: "The true mark of a saved man is not that he wants to go to heaven" but instead "that he is willing to go to China, or to Labrador, to the battlefield of France, or to the slums of a great city" so he can participate in building "the kingdom of God on earth."[4]

Some on the second side make the rather audacious claim that those who spend their time thinking about a far-off Heaven will fail to engage culture and the world already near to them. But those who make this claim know nothing of the facts. C. S. Lewis once said, "If you read history you will find that the Christians who did most for the present world were just those who thought most of the next."[5] I fear that more often than not, what the critics are really saying is that they themselves think this Christian belief about Heaven is tomfoolery.

Those with enough sense to watch what is happening in the noisy, cheer-filled gym need to ask for a moment of silence to announce that there is no reason why we can't live for now in light of Heaven. Too much focus on the future Heaven or on life in the here and now misses the dual emphasis of the Bible—and indeed of our lives. Heaven people ought to be the most zealous about care for creation, love of others, peacemaking, and social justice. Heaven people have tasted the grandeur of Heaven, and therefore they long for Heaven to begin its work now on earth. But these same active workers can also be those who long the most for the fullness of God's presence and the perfection of God's people in the new Heavens and the new earth.

How then should Heaven people live now? Let's get one thing clear first, if it isn't already obvious: to be Heaven people we don't need to be heroes. Heaven people live ordinary lives in ordinary places with ordinary families. They work at ordinary vocations. Eugene Peterson has exhorted his readers to practice the resurrection in the here and now. The practicing of resurrection on earth is tied to the heart of the Heaven Promise: the resurrection of Jesus. Here is how Peterson poetically stated it:

Jesus was radically reconfigured and redefined by resurrection. And now [the disciples] were being just as radically reconfigured and redefined by resurrection.[6]

To practice resurrection now means permitting our morning, our midday, our evening, and our night to be redefined by resurrection. Everything having to do with everything we do and everything we are can be swallowed into resurrection life.

Yes, it is true. Some people are so Heavenly minded they are no earthly good, but the opposite is just as often or even far more often the case. One of my friends, Joe Stowell, in his wonderful book *Eternity,* sketched out the impact of eternity for life today. As a good preacher, he alliterated the list: posture toward God, possessions, perception of people, perspective on pain, pleasures on earth, and a new kind of purity.[7] I shall offer now my own list in light of all that has been said above about the Heaven Promise, the heart of the promise, and the major features of the promise in the new Heavens and the new earth.

HEAVEN PEOPLE TRUST

The affirmative response to a contract is a signature, to an invitation an acceptance, to a covenant a commitment, and to a promise trust. God promised Heaven, and he made that promise alive and real in the resurrection of Jesus. But we are called to trust this promising God in our daily lives. We do this in how we live and how we die. Some days we walk in a vibrant faith and other days, like Peter, we begin to sink into waters of doubt.

Like the father who longed for his son to be healed, we may need to cry out in the presence of God: "I do believe; help me overcome my unbelief!"* We are not promised that in trusting God we will experience constant, victorious, abounding faith. What is promised—and please don't forget this—is that God will be faithful to his Heaven Promise.

What encourages our faith the most is to turn to Jesus, to face Jesus, to listen to Jesus, and to watch Jesus. Open your Bible to any of the Gospels and begin reading. You will see Jesus, and if you keep reading, you will see Jesus go through it all: joys and sorrows, commitments and betrayals, birth and growth, and life and death. But if you keep reading to the last page of any of the Gospels, you will encounter the

---

* Mark 9:24

resurrected Jesus. Stand in the empty tomb with him and face your past, your present, and your future in light of the resurrection of Jesus.

Trusting looks different for each of us. For the young adult, for the young mother and father, for the career person—single or married—for the retiring person, for the elderly, and for the widower or widow. For some, trusting will mean being faithful under pressure; for some it will mean disciplining rough edges; for others it will mean waiting, sometimes in pain and sometimes alone. But trusting is a genuine mark of Heaven people.

HEAVEN PEOPLE IMAGINE

Heaven people ought to be the emperors of imagination. Once we catch a glimpse of what God plans for the kingdom, we can begin to implement that vision in the here and now—beginning in our churches and in our homes and in our worship. Timothy Williamson has written about the power (and danger) of imagination:

> Imagination can change the world because it is a means to knowledge, and
> knowledge can change the world. Imagination can change the world for
> better and for worse, because knowledge can.[8]

Williamson is on to something, and it reverberates through the souls of many of us because of MercyMe's song called "I Can Only Imagine." The band asks questions about what Heaven will be like—about the heart's sensations, about expressing our joys, about how we will worship—and concludes we can't really know but we can imagine.

Let us agree that imagination is a God-given power that can be unleashed to bring Heaven to earth in the here and now. This is where our sketch of the big ideas about Heaven can both contain and excite our imagination. What will the new Heavens and new earth be like? God will be all in all, Jesus will be in the center, and we will enter into an eternal utopia of joy, happiness, and pleasure. Life will blow away the dust of death, and we will discover an eternal global fellowship in God's beloved community. Heaven people imagine those sorts of things in advance in worship: making God central to life, giving Jesus the lordship and honor he deserves, pursuing happiness as God designs, facing death standing in the empty tomb, and working to resolve the breakdowns of all racial, ethnic, social, cultural, and sexual divisions. Heaven people focus on a society marked by love, justice, peace, and wisdom.

What will that look like? Heaven people know that all earthly power, no matter how good or how evil, is time-stamped for the day God, the All in All, will reign for forever and beyond. The day is coming when powers will surrender once and forever to the Lamb-shaped Throne of God. Heaven people live and worship in the now in light of the hope of the Lamb's victory over sin and evil. Heaven people imagine life with God on the Throne.

I like the life that monks lead, not because I want to be a monk, but because their schedule speaks to how God is the center of their lives. The monk's life is punctuated, in the Benedictine's case, seven times per day with prayer and listening to Scripture read. Every day for a Benedictine shifts from work to prayer and Word, and from Word and prayer back to work. God didn't call me to the monastic life, but the monastic life is a symbol of what God wants for each of us: to allow the sacred rhythms of prayer and worship to shape the entire day. We orient our hearts toward God, toward the Lamb, when our days are punctuated with times for Word and prayer. Heaven people have imaginations that are enthused by contemplation on the Word and by prayer.

A Slight Digression Within Imagine

One word about worship. When we worship God, we are declaring our true allegiance. When we worship God, we are simultaneously not worshiping Caesar, the empire, the politics of our day, the power of greed and money, or the seductiveness of sensualities. When we worship, we say no to the Beast of Babylon. To worship God is a protest of the world as well as an orientation of the world toward its true God. Heaven people imagine a world worshiping God.

One word about the Lamb. The way of the Lamb is the way of a life that ended in a pitiful, painful death. But it also is the way of a death-defeating resurrection that snapped forever the jaws of death. Heaven people orient themselves toward a life shaped by life, death, and resurrection. Not just living life; not obsessed with the sufferings of Christ; and not just thinking positively of the resurrection. Heaven people love life, know the reality of suffering, pain, and death, yet live through death into the kingdom of God by the power of the resurrection. Heaven people imagine a world enthralled by the way of the Lamb.

One word about the Spirit. Heaven people live in the power of the unleashed Spirit, and this Spirit, to quote the words of James D. G. Dunn, "transcends human ability and transforms human inability."[9] Heaven people know God's Spirit is at work in God's planting of the Spirit in our spirits, in the outpouring of the Spirit throughout the world, in anointing people to exercise gifts and fruit and leadership, and in liberating people from whatever holds them in bondage.[10] Heaven people invoke God's Spirit to fill them, even as they imagine a world filled with God's unleashed Spirit.

And a final word about how we order our lives. God gave a calendar to ancient Israel to order their lives. They were called to enter into the great moments of God's redemption: the new year of hope, the Passover of liberation, the exodus into the giving of the Law and the entry into the Land, the Day of Atonement, and the dedication of the temple. Each year, every observant Jew relived the story of Israel in order to remember what God had done. This remembering evoked faith and taught the Jews how to live in the present *and* the future in light of that calendar's events.

The church then adjusted the calendar to focus on the events of Jesus's life. Anticipation and Jesus's birth (Advent and Christmas), his appearing (Epiphany), anticipating his death and resurrection and ascension (Lent, Holy Week, Good Friday, Easter), Pentecost, and Ordinary Time, when we focus on big themes in the life and teachings of Jesus. Heaven people, whether they observe this calendar or not, orient their lives toward Jesus so that his life becomes their life and their life becomes his life in them. Heaven people imagine a world shaped by a calendar focused on Jesus.

HEAVEN PEOPLE PLANT AND BUILD

Heaven people do not dreamily escape from this world. Instead, to each of us is given a task, a calling, a vocation—whatever it might be—and each of us is to do that task. Dietrich Bonhoeffer was teaching the illegal seminary for preachers in Finkenwalde (now a part of Poland) while contemplating his involvement in a conspiracy to bring down Hitler and his evil system. In a meditation on Psalm 119, he said:

> The earth that feeds me has a right to my work and my strength. . . . I may
> not evade my destiny to be a guest and stranger [on earth] . . . by dreaming
> away my earthly life with thoughts about heaven.[11]

Heaven people have an earthly life to which they are committed, to the glory of God. Why? In the first chapter of the Bible, God interprets his own work with a word that needs to be pasted on the door of every church. The word is *good*. The light was good, the land was good, vegetation (surely God means strawberries) was good, the sun and moon are good, all creatures great and small (not the exact words, of course) in the waters and on the land are good, and then God made a male and female in his own image. When he was all done, God said it was "very good." God's own interpretation of his creation is that it is very good. In the goodness of God's creation we begin to see how Heaven people live. Heaven people dwell in God's good creation and are summoned by God to a task to govern this world under God for his glory.

There is a legend that Martin Luther once said, "Even if I knew that tomorrow the world would go to pieces, I would still plant my apple tree."[12] There is no evidence Luther ever said that, but it's still true: by planting an apple tree, we go about our calling. Our calling is to do well what we have been called to do, and that calling is an earthly calling (for now). Christian wisdom has led us all to see that God grants to each of us a place in the sun, and Heaven people bask in the place God grants them.

Elizabeth Achtemeier, a wonderful Bible scholar and preacher, put this into perspective when speaking about our need to be faithful to our gifts. She wrapped it all in God's Heaven Promise:

> God takes the little gifts of excellence and hope and faith that we have and
> the little contributions of beauty and that love that we make, and he brings
> them all to perfection in a kingdom that will not pass away.[13]

Do what you are called to do, do it well, and do it with an eye on exercising your gifts forever and ever in the new Heavens and new earth.

HEAVEN PEOPLE MAKE THINGS RIGHT

The core of the Heaven Promise is that in the new Heavens and the earth, *God will make all things right*. Each word matters: *God* will do this; *will make* is the promise; *all things* means all things—all people, all actions, all systems; and *right* means God promises that the earth in its new-creation form will run as God designed it to run.

Heaven people *begin to make things right, now,* on earth.

A confession. As a high school sophomore, I had a cool hippie teacher for English class. He had long hair, and he asked us to call him by his first name. Plus, he didn't lecture. Like us, he sat in a chair, and we all sat in the round looking at one another and doing our best to engage in conversations that our teacher—I'll call him Mr. Hippie—created. One of Mr. Hippie's ideas was freedom, which he wanted to run throughout the class. One result is that he was negotiable when it came to assignments. Instead of requiring us to read a canon of classics in the Western tradition (such as Milton and Hemingway), he gave us freedom to go to the library and read what we wanted. He asked us to write two book reviews for the class, and I chose Willa Cather's *O Pioneers!* and *My Antonia.* I had never heard of the author, and I'm pretty sure Mr. Hippie had not read the books.

Now, for the confession: I was an athlete who was busy after school, and when I had time, I had a girlfriend, Kris (who is now my lovely wife), and the deadline for reading those two books was about to come. I chose to invent plots and summaries and descriptions and critical interaction. Mr. Hippie gave me a B or a B+, which was what he usually gave me on my assignments. Evidently, he had no idea what those books were about (and neither did I).

Then between my junior and senior years in high school, I got right with God. One of the first things I did was to write Mr. Hippie a letter, telling him what I had done and why. I wanted to confess it as sin because as a Christian I didn't want that weighing against me for all eternity. My father was also a teacher, and he ran into Mr. Hippie just after my teacher read my letter. Mr. Hippie told my dad he had not seen anything like that in all his (three or four) years of teaching. My dad told me Mr. Hippie was proud of my honesty.

I bumped into Mr. Hippie later in the hallway. He pulled me aside and told me how much he appreciated what I had confessed. I was expecting the hammer to fall, afraid in part that I might get flunked for that course and have to retake the class. But I also knew he was a hippie and that it was more likely he'd find a creative solution. Which he did: he forgave me and told me that I needed, someday, to read those books by Willa Cather.

Which I did in the summer and fall of 2014! They are great books, and every night I sat down to read, I was glad that I had made that matter right with God and with my hippie teacher.

In Heaven God will make all things right. The God who promises us that kind of Heaven is at work in us now to infect the world with making things right everywhere we go.

HEAVEN PEOPLE FELLOWSHIP WITH OTHERS INTO GOD'S BELOVED COMMUNITY

The Bible's vision of Heaven is a vision of God's people surrounding the Throne and the Lamb in praise, worship, and service. Heaven is not made for everyone, sadly. Not everyone wants Heaven. Heaven is made for God's Heaven people.

"There are," C. S. Lewis famously wrote in *The Great Divorce*, "only two kinds of people in the end: those who say to God, 'Thy will be done,' and those to whom God says in the end, '*Thy* will be done.'"[14] Since Heaven is for "God's will be done" people, Heaven people enter now into fellowship with other "God's will be done" people. They are drawn now into the family and fellowship of the church — the people who are faithfully serving as they faithfully wait for Heaven.

Yes, we are talking church as in church universal and church local. Church is designed to embody, in advance, what will happen in Heaven. In Heaven, God's people will love, worship, and serve God. Heaven people begin those acts now: they love God now, they worship God now, and they serve God now. If Heaven is a world of love, as Jonathan Edwards liked to say, if Heaven is a world of reconciled people, if Heaven is a world of justice and peace, then Heaven people are to live a life marked by love of others, reconciled relationships, and a life oriented toward justice and peace.

Heaven then is both theocentric and kingdom-centric, and its being kingdom-centric means we are called to live as Heaven people by developing the character of those fit for that kind of Heaven. We are to commit now to a world that looks like that kind of Heaven. If the final Heaven is an eternal global fellowship, Heaven people are not so nationalistic that they hate other countries. Why? They know in every country there is a connection that is tighter than national or ethnic ties. If the final Heaven is an eternal, beloved community where racism and classism and ethnic hierarchies end, then they live that kind of beloved community with one another now.

In saying that Heaven people fellowship with others, I am gathering together all I said in two previous chapters having to do with the global fellowship and God's beloved community. But this time we are looking at things positively: instead of the "no more" themes about injustice and violence, we now see that the final Heaven will be marked by fellowship, love, grace, and reconciliation. Heaven people seek to embody that kind of fellowship now—crossing borders and boundaries—because of the unleashed power of the Resurrection available to us.

You might wonder how this can be done. Let's ask the big question: What is the kingdom like as a society? It will be a society marked by love, by justice, by holiness, and by peace. "Now go therefore and do that." In the context of your local church, practice love and justice and holiness and peace.

HEAVEN PEOPLE FORGIVE

Earlier I told part of the story of Leslie Leyland Fields and her sister Laurie, a story wracked by the pain of abusive parenting and neglect. If in the first hour of the final Heaven we all are reconciled with God and with one another, Heaven people are to begin that process now. That is what the Leyland children have attempted. Leslie's question is their question: "How can I forgive him [their abusive father] for all the years past?" That is the question Heaven people ask now and the one they begin answering now. Her father, so far as I can tell, never mentioned Leslie's name when she visited with him a number of times later in life, but she and her siblings know that "forgiveness is strong enough to break generational sins."[15]

Theirs is a story of offering forgiveness to a barely comprehending, sometimes rejecting, and sometimes slightly embracing father. The siblings once found a home to rent in Florida in which to entertain their father. As Leslie describes it,

> We welcomed him among us, offered the best chair we had, the best food we had bought. We put a robe on his lap. We made a party for a man who hardly laughs, who did not show love for us, our love spilling over, multiplying in the rooms and at the table, like loaves and fishes.[16]

But Laurie's story maps forgiveness, and Leslie describes how her abused sister and her brother Clark were with their father when he died:

> To Laurie, he looked like a little boy, helpless, his hair disheveled in sleep. They read scriptures to him. Laurie stroked his hair, his head, told him she loved him, that it was okay for him to go now. . . . She thought of all he had done, how he had used her as a girl. She wanted to wipe away those years. She hated him for how her life had gone for so many years after because of him, but there was love too. He had asked for her forgiveness two years before in a phone call. He'd told her she was a beautiful person inside and out; she had a wonderful heart; he loved her, and would she forgive him? She had said yes.[17]

Now she was attending to her dying father, a father who had wrecked her life in many ways. "The abused loved the abuser and made sure he had a bed at night, meals every day, gifts at Christmas, and phone calls when he was alone, though he had done none of this for her, for any of us." Then he passed. "Laurie sat in a kind of shock. Numb, she fixed his hair, folded his hands across his chest, kissed him on the cheek, and prayed he was with the Lord."[18]

Heaven people live now in light of a Heaven shaped by reconciliation, no matter how difficult and impossible it may seem.

Heaven People Melt Snow

Narnia, you may remember, was kept in snow by the White Witch, the usurping ruler who surely knew who the rightful king really was—Aslan. Wherever Aslan enters into the land, the snows begin to melt as if spring were arriving. Aslan is captured and put to death on the Stone Table, but the White Witch does not know there is an ancient formula at work: when an innocent victim voluntarily surrenders to the powers of the witch, her powers are broken and healing begins to work in reverse. The Stone Table cracks, the lion comes back to life, and Aslan breaks into the White Witch's castle. Once there, he breathes life into those who have been frozen.

That is a wonderful image of what happens in the final Heaven: the snow of evil and systemic injustice and nonreconciliation will melt under the illuminating grace of the Lamb on the Throne.

But we are not to wait until then to get the snow melting. We are called, now, to melt the snows of our own lives.

When the final Heaven's saints are known, surely one of the more infamous saints of the twentieth century will be Brennan Manning. In his own summary of his life:

> Mine has been anything but a straight shot, more like a crooked path filled
> with thorns and crows and vodka. Prone to wander? You bet. I've been a
> priest, then an ex-priest. Husband, then ex-husband. Amazed crowds one
> night and lied to friends the next. Drunk for years, sober for a season, then
> drunk again. I've been John the beloved, Peter the coward, and Thomas the
> doubter all before the waitress brought the check.[19]

When I read his memoir, *All Is Grace,* I grieved over the snowy hardness and distance of his mother and father and how it stained and shaped Brennan's life. To them he was one big disappointment. As Manning told it, he lived with a snowed-in "sense of being completely insufficient as a person," and their veneer of a Catholic faith imposed on Manning the idea that God was "Something Awful." I grieved over Manning's having turned to alcohol at such a young age and how that alcohol

controlled far too much of his life, even as he shared with others God's uncondi-
tional love and grace. He was often snowed-in personally while melting snow in the
lives of others. I rejoiced over his discovery of God in Christ and of his powerful
mystical encounter with God. But the man struggled mightily with his own belief,
the belief he shared with thousands, that God really did love him. There were cracks
of light that melted the snow in his heart, like the time when a fellow priest told him
that "It's okay not to be okay."[20]

But what most strikes the reader is what happened when his mother died. When
given the sad news over the phone, his first response was, *"God, what a bother."* He
flew to Newark and found a motel near the church where the funeral would be held.

> I stopped at a liquor store before checking in and bought a quart of their
> cheapest Scotch. While others arranged flowers . . . I locked the door of my
> room, pulled the curtains, and drank. . . . Like a good alcoholic, I kept
> drinking and drinking and drinking.[21]

Manning missed his mother's funeral. That's a sad story, but one that somehow
turned toward snow-melting grace. About a decade after his mother's death, while
praying, Manning's mother's face flashed across his mind. Here is how he describes
this moment of reaching into God's heavenly grace:

> I saw my mother as a little six-year-old girl kneeling on the windowsill of [her]
> orphanage in Montreal. Her nose was pressed against the glass; she was
> begging God to send her a mommy and daddy who would whisk her away
> and love her without condition. As I looked, I believe I finally *saw* my
> mother; she was a ragamuffin too. And all my resentment and anger fell away.
>
> The little girl turned and walked toward me . . . and she stood before me
> as an aged woman. She said, "You know, I messed up a lot when you were a
> kid. But you turned out okay." Then my mother did something she'd never
> done before in her life, never once. She kissed me on the lips and on both
> cheeks. At that moment I knew the hurt between my mother and me was real
> and did matter, but it was okay. The trusting heart gives a second chance; it is

forgiven and, in turn, forgives. I looked at my mother and said, "I forgive you."[22]

QUESTIONS, QUESTIONS

One cannot sketch the Heaven promises without having questions, and I have done my best to avoid conversations about *all* those questions. I want now to turn to some of the questions, but here is the important thing:

> We must approach each question in light of the major features of the Heaven Promise, focusing on the big picture and not getting lost in curiosities and questions that cannot be contained by the Bible's words.

So let's review the big ideas:

First, God gave us our imaginations, but the surest place for understanding Heaven is not our imaginations or stories of afterlife experiences, but the Bible itself.

Second, Heaven is God's promise to us, and it is as good as God is sure. We are to trust our good God if we want to inherit the Heaven Promise.

Third, the heart of the Heaven Promise is that God raised Jesus from the dead, and the resurrected One had a real body fit for the new Heavens and the new earth. Our hope is for the resurrection and that kind of eternal, glorified, and transformed body.

Fourth, there are two heavens in the Bible: the present heaven, which is where God is. This heaven is just beyond our gaze. Then there is the final Heaven, or the new Heavens and the new earth.

Fifth, the final Heaven has these themes: God will be All in All, Jesus will be Jesus in the middle of it all, everyone will love God and love others eternally, Heaven will be a utopia of pleasures, Heaven will be eternal life, and Heaven will be an eternal beloved community.

The many questions that we hear about Heaven can distract us sometimes from these five central themes. But if we keep these in mind, I'm confident we can arrive at good answers to questions that we all ask.

Part Four

TEN QUESTIONS ABOUT HEAVEN

We turn now to ten questions about heaven. I have no desire to rank them in the order of their importance or in the order of frequency with which they are asked. The most important question is the question you have, and I hope I have touched on your question in what we have discussed already, or in what follows. Some of the chapters that follow are longer than others, but that is because of the complexity of the questions. I begin with near-death experiences because nearly everyone seems to ask about them.

What About
Near-Death Experiences?

An Old Theme Suddenly New

It's as hard to explain away testimonies of near-death
experiences as it is to explain them.

— Arthur Roberts

What about all the reports about near-death and out-of-body experiences?* Are they the brain's "last hurrah," as some scientists (would like to) think,[1] or are they more than that?

How do we understand *Heaven Is for Real,* the movie about the little boy who is said to have died and come back? Are such stories factual? Do they reveal anything about the afterlife? Do they prove there is a heaven or a hell? Do they give us genuine glimpses into the next life?

Arthur Roberts, a philosopher, has said it well: "It's as hard to explain away testimonies of near-death experiences as it is to explain them"![2] He is flanked by another philosopher, Jerry Walls, who after writing a long and patient chapter

---

* Often called NDEs and OBEs.

(the sort philosophers write) to the book *Heaven,* concluded that NDEs "deserve serious consideration as positive evidence for the Christian doctrine of heaven."[3]

After reading at least one hundred NDE or OBE accounts, I happened to be reading some lines written by the apostle Paul. It occurred to me that following one of his brutal persecutions, he might have had a near-death experience. Here are Paul's words, and if you are a reader of NDE or OBE accounts, you can be forgiven for wondering if Paul's experience should be included among those reports:

> I know a man in Christ who fourteen years ago was caught up to the third heaven. Whether it was in the body or out of the body I do not know—God knows. And I know that this man—whether in the body or apart from the body I do not know, but God knows—was caught up to paradise and heard inexpressible things, things that no one is permitted to tell.[*]

And what about Stephen who, in the act of being stoned to death by his enemies had nothing short of a visionary experience that is not far from what some encounter in an NDE:

> But Stephen, full of the Holy Spirit, looked up to heaven and saw the glory of God, and Jesus standing at the right hand of God. "Look," he said, "I see heaven open and the Son of Man standing at the right hand of God." . . .
>
> While they were stoning him, Stephen prayed, "Lord Jesus, receive my spirit." Then he fell on his knees and cried out, "Lord, do not hold this sin against them." When he had said this, he fell asleep.[†]

Was either of these, or both of these, an NDE? I don't know. But the words in these passages sound like what I have read in stories of NDEs.

Even if we think Paul and Stephen had an NDE or an OBE, a problem remains. There is so much variety in these stories that a careful listener can easily come away

---

* 2 Corinthians 12:2–4
† Acts 7:55–56, 59–60

totally confused. So what can we learn? After studying these stories, I believe they are *glimpses* of the afterlife. But I also believe we need to be wary of making the claim that they reveal what Heaven will be like.

NEAR-DEATH EXPERIENCES: THE TYPICAL STORY

An expert on NDEs, Mally Cox-Chapman, informs us that a Gallup poll once reported some 8 million Americans have had such experiences. Cox-Chapman's research into NDEs discovered the most common elements of an NDE:

- Feelings of peace and quiet
- Feeling oneself out of the body
- Going through a dark tunnel
- Meeting others, including one or more beings of light
- A life review
- Coming to a border or limit
- Coming back
- Seeing life differently
- Having new views of death

Cox-Chapman reached four conclusions. First, the experiencers become believers in some kind of life after death: "If experiencers were atheists before, they are believers [in the afterlife] afterward." Second, they become more universalistic in their faith. As she puts it, "If they had a firm commitment to one particular religion before, they believe any religious path leads to God afterward." Third, they believe in the afterlife. Cox-Chapman: "They say they absolutely believe that their souls will persist beyond physical death." Fourth, Cox-Chapman believes on the basis of her study that "we will be provided with the Heaven that is right for each of us."[4]

Which reminds me of what Lisa Miller said of Alice Sebold, author of *The Lovely Bones,* a national bestseller about heaven: "The guiding principle in [my conception of heaven] is that it's inclusive: it allows you to have what you want and what you desire." When asked the reason behind her thinking, Sebold said, "I've always felt that there were so many rules and exclusions out there in conceptions of redemption and the afterlife—it didn't include me and a lot of my friends."[5]

This brings us back to the question, *How do we know what Heaven is really like?* For many people, stories of NDEs and OBEs have become what Cox-Chapman calls a "source of contemporary revelation" leading to "a new age in consciousness."

Perhaps the more important conclusion Cox-Chapman draws has to do with the effect of these stories on a person's faith. "Churchgoers," she wrote, "all seemed to outgrow church in favor of more self-directed and universalist beliefs."[6]

NDEs, then, do not prove the Heaven that Jesus or Paul or the Bible teach. In fact, I would be prepared to argue that if each NDE is a genuine encounter with the real afterlife, with what many today would call heaven, *then the Christian faith is but one path and Jesus was seriously mistaken* when he said, "No one comes to the Father *except* through me."* We have to wonder if NDEs are little more than a case of people projecting onto eternity what they want for themselves. Or maybe the stories provide little more than a glimpse of the afterlife. The odd thing is that if some of those who experience an NDE or an OBE do come away with a more universal religious faith, others discover a much deeper confirmation of their *Christian* faith and their stories are found all over the Christian Inspiration bookshelves.

What are we to make of the specifically Christian near-death experiences? Are we guilty of liking the NDE stories that confirm our faith but disliking the ones that don't? Is it right to affirm one and denounce the other collection of these stories?

WHAT SHOULD WE THINK?

It's obvious that NDEs vary wildly, and that's why we need to explore this theme again. What we need is a history of these experiences, since this history makes it clear that the reports are *interpretations*, and the interpretations reflect the beliefs of the one undergoing the experience. An NDE expresses what the person already believes. I'm not denying the experience or its impact. But the *interpretation* of that experience flows out of what one already thinks. In fact, this is proven by studying history.

Carol Zaleski studied what she called "otherworld journeys" in the ancient world among the Greeks, Egyptians, and Romans before she turned to the Bible and

---

* John 14:6

then to the history of the church. Her conclusions jar my confidence that today's NDEs report accurate information. There may be some similarities in the stories (tunnels, darkness, the presence of a guide, a warm light, and so on), but there also are so many notable differences that one has to conclude that *different eras tell different stories about NDEs.*[7] We must ask: Do the era-related differences suggest these stories have far more to do with the time period and the culture than some kind of reality beyond death?

To the discomfort of Protestants, the vision of the afterlife among the medievals included the Blessed Virgin Mary, and those who lived in Middle Ages experienced purgatory and hell far more often than those who report NDEs today. The fact that this element of NDEs today goes unreported or underreported skews what people think about the afterlife, which then shapes what they experience in an NDE! In Zaleski's view, the fatal flaw in the modern NDE account is that it is *"through and through a work of the socially conditioned religious imagination."* Notice those words carefully: NDEs emerge from a *socially conditioned imagination.* Therefore, she concludes, "we can no longer insist that [well-known books about these experiences] or any other work of visionary eschatology paints a true picture of what occurs at the extreme border of life."[8]

Try this as an experiment. In the same week, read Eben Alexander's *Proof of Heaven* and then Marvin Besteman's *My Journey to Heaven.* After finishing both books you will wonder if these authors are talking about the same heaven. The former has God asking to be called Om, and the latter meets none other than Saint Peter at the gates of Heaven. Some of these stories boldly affirm that all will be saved, while others, like Sid Roth's *Heaven Is Beyond Your Wildest Experiences: Ten True Stories of Experiencing Heaven* or Colton Burpo's *Heaven Is for Real,* reveal salvation as a reality only for those who have faith in Christ.

But if you were to read, say, the NDE of Carl Jung, famous for inventing Jungian psychology, you will discover a very, well, Jungian afterlife. And if we familiarize ourselves with pious Jewish visions of heaven, we discover a heaven filled with music shaped by how the rabbis understood and glorified the Torah.[9] Or, as a famous collection of pious, Hasidic stories, called *In Praise of the Baal Shem Tov,* says, "In early days when people revived after lying in a coma close to death, they used to tell about the awesome things they had seen in the upper world."[10] All to say this: every religious, ethnic, and cultural group has stories to tell. The overlaps between those who have NDEs are worthy of serious study, but the differences among the various stories over the course of history are so dramatic it makes me skeptical that they are reporting what Heaven or the afterlife is like.

Not only that, but the Christian who wants to shape his or her view of Heaven on the basis of the Bible has to observe that the NDEs of today differ quite noticeably from what is found in the Bible in passages such as Revelation 20–22. In NDE stories, God often is not the center; Jesus is not the Savior or the Lord or the King; there is very little about devotion to God or a society marked by justice and fellowship. The absence of the major biblical themes make me doubly wary that near-death experiences reveal anything about Heaven.

Can we learn from the NDEs and the OBEs? Perhaps. NDEs and OBEs provide a cautious affirmation that life continues after death but hardly make a foolproof case for the experience of heaven. After studying NDEs as pastors, James Garlow and Keith Wall arrived at some responsible conclusions. They think God in his grace grants some people glimpses of heaven.[11] I agree, but I want to phrase it slightly differently: near-death experiences are glimpses of *an afterlife*. I believe not only in an afterlife but in Heaven. I don't believe in Heaven on the basis that people have been there and come back. I believe in Heaven because God promised Heaven and because Jesus was raised from the dead.

What About Rewards in Heaven?

What Grace Creates Remains Grace

> When evening came, the owner of the vineyard said to his
> foreman, "Call the workers and pay them their wages,
> beginning with the last ones hired and going on to the first."
>
> — Jesus

Will some people be happier than others? Will the pleasure of some be more intense than that of others? Will we all experience God and one another and Heaven to the same degree? Will some of us be closer to God than others? Will anyone have a higher status than others?

And what about rewards in Heaven and the Bible's talk about "crowns"? Will we all be equals, or will some be more equal than others?

Let's face the very common American cultural problem first. According to Peter Kreeft, we are for some reason instinctively egalitarians when it comes to Heaven:

> We modern egalitarians are tempted to the primal sin of pride in the opposite
> way from the ancients. The old, aristocratic form of pride was the desire to be
> better than others. The new, democratic form is the desire not to have anyone
> better than yourself.[1]

To respond to Kreeft's point, if this were Twitter, we would tag this comment #boom. He's right, and we need to make up our minds on the basis of what the Bible reveals, not on the basis of our culture's preferences.

When I was a boy attending Sunday school, on the wall behind the teacher hung a set of red ribbons. At the top of each ribbon were names in my gender-separated class: Bobby, Bruce, Kelvin, Mike, Scot, and so on. Each ribbon was about one foot long, seemingly snipped at the end at an angle with pinking shears. Our teacher had a supply of small one-and-a-half-inch paper medallions for those who memorized Bible verses or whole chapters of the Bible or time-honored hymns and poems. Most of the time the ribbons hung without alterations, but every now and then the competitive fires would heat up. Suddenly, a number of us would start memorizing. One time I came in with both a Bible verse and a hymn.

The theory behind the ribbons was that if we motivate (sometimes competitively) children to memorize important Bible passages—such as the Ten Commandments, Psalm 23, the Beatitudes of Jesus, the Love Chapter in 1 Corinthians 13—the Word of God would begin to impact the children. Which it did, no doubt. But what it did more of was light our competitive fires. I wanted to claim the longest ribbon, so I memorized and practiced and recited and then came back for more. Before long I had a second ribbon and, if my memory serves me right, I may have had a third ribbon . . . on which hung but one medallion. Then, when no one challenged my ribbon, I shifted into cruise control. Having the longest ribbon was a bit of an honor (if only at church).

It was not unusual for the Sunday school teacher to connect our ribbons with our rewards in Heaven. It's important for us to think about this because I, for one, was motivated by heavenly rewards due to my competitive nature. Ezra Stiles, a famous early-American pastor and president of Yale College, preached and taught often about heavenly rewards. He would emphasize the *intensity* view of rewards—in other words, he appealed to eternal pleasure. In his words, "Every good work individuals did on earth . . . would increase their heavenly reward. Every soul they helped save would enhance their eternal happiness and enable them to shine with 'a more distinguished luster through eternal ages.'"[2]

What are we to think? Would it be Heaven if my Sunday school reward system suddenly became eternal? Would it be fair or unfair?

Jesus Reveals That It Is All Grace and Not About Fairness

Let's begin with Jesus. I need to quote an entire parable so we can catch the drift of what Jesus was getting at when it comes to rewards.* The story begins with a common scene: an estate owner hired day laborers.

> For the kingdom of heaven is like a landowner who went out early in the morning to hire workers for his vineyard. He agreed to pay them a denarius for the day and sent them into his vineyard.
>
> About nine in the morning he went out and saw others standing in the marketplace doing nothing. He told them, "You also go and work in my vineyard, and I will pay you whatever is right." So they went.
>
> He went out again about noon and about three in the afternoon and did the same thing. About five in the afternoon he went out and found still others standing around. He asked them, "Why have you been standing here all day long doing nothing?"
>
> "Because no one has hired us," they answered.
>
> He said to them, "You also go and work in my vineyard."

Then the owner called them all in for their pay, but the owner's actions were uncustomary, perhaps unjust, and upsetting:

> When evening came, the owner of the vineyard said to his foreman, "Call the workers and pay them their wages, beginning with the last ones hired and going on to the first."
>
> The workers who were hired about five in the afternoon came and each

* Matthew 20:1–16

received a denarius. So when those came who were hired first, they expected to receive more. But each one of them also received a denarius. When they received it, they began to grumble against the landowner. "These who were hired last worked only one hour," they said, "and you have made them equal to us who have borne the burden of the work and the heat of the day."

The owner had evidently changed the game.

But he answered one of them, "I am not being unfair to you, friend. Didn't you agree to work for a denarius? Take your pay and go. I want to give the one who was hired last the same as I gave you. Don't I have the right to do what I want with my own money? Or are you envious because I am generous?"

So the last will be first, and the first will be last.

What a strange business method the owner had. R. T. France, a Matthew scholar, put it this way: "Any union leader worth their salt would protest at such employment practices."[3] Let's agree that Jesus is not revising economic systems on earth as much as teaching an economy of the kingdom.

His fundamental idea is that in the kingdom, *the correlation between work and reward is out of whack.* Jesus wants us to feel sympathy for those who worked more but got paid the same amount as others who worked fewer hours. Why? So we will realize that God's ways are not our ways. God is generous, while we are exacting. The parable is not about reversing the order, but instead about the end to ordering.

The whole parable comes down to the question that we read just ahead of the last line: "Or are you envious because I am generous?" Human envy is the opposite of divine generosity. God's generosity is not like our desire for order, rank, status, and hierarchy. In Heaven, God will be God, Jesus will be on the Throne, and we will all *equally* be gazing at God in his glory (not ours).

CROWNS ARE METAPHORS
FOR GOD'S GRACIOUS WORK IN US

What about the passages that refer to a crown? Don't they teach a system of rewards, status, and hierarchy that exists in Heaven? Five different rewards are mentioned in the Bible:*

> Blessed is the one who perseveres under trial because, having stood the test, that person will receive *the crown of life* that the Lord has promised to those who love him.
>
> For what is our hope, our joy, or *the crown in which we will glory* in the presence of our Lord Jesus when he comes? Is it not you?
>
> Everyone who competes in the games goes into strict training. They do it to get a crown that will not last, but we do it to get *a crown that will last forever.* Therefore I do not run like someone running aimlessly; I do not fight like a boxer beating the air. No, I strike a blow to my body and make it my slave so that after I have preached to others, I myself will not be disqualified for the prize.
>
> Now there is in store for me *the crown of righteousness,* which the Lord, the righteous Judge, will award to me on that day—and not only to me, but also to all who have longed for his appearing.
>
> Be shepherds of God's flock that is under your care, watching over them—not because you must, but because you are willing, as God wants you to be; not pursuing dishonest gain, but eager to serve; not lording it over those entrusted to you, but being examples to the flock. And when the Chief Shepherd appears, you will receive *the crown of glory that will never fade away.*

In this set of verses, Jesus seems to be saying the opposite of what he said in the parable of the workers described just prior to these crown metaphors. In these

---

* James 1:12 (see also Revelation 2:10; 3:11); 1 Thessalonians 2:19; 1 Corinthians 9:25–27; 2 Timothy 4:8; 1 Peter 5:2–4

passages we notice a strict correlation between what we do—persevere, pastoral ministry, spiritual disciplining of the body, longing for Christ to return, and being a good example—and what we get (a crown to honor what we do). And in addition to the crown passages, we find important passages about rewards, all of them wrapped up in a simple statement by the apostle Paul:*

> For we must all appear before the judgment seat of Christ, so that each of us may receive what is due us [*rewards*] for the things done while in the body, whether good or bad.

Is there a way to put these together? I think so. Here are the big ideas about rewards:

First, all talk of reward (or of our status or our capacities to enjoy God) distracts from God's glory and the promise that we will experience intense, satisfying pleasures forever more.

Second, there is no talk of gradations in heaven in John's book of Revelation. Read his last visions in Revelation 20–22 with this in mind, and you'll see that no one is more important than anyone else.

Third, it is far wiser to see the language of reward as God's way of motivating us to be faithful. The impact of this language, I know at least for me, is to motivate me to be more faithful.

Here is the point: all saints will be full of joy and you can't be fuller than full.[4] God's generosity will overwhelm any sense of correlation between what we have done on earth and any reward in Heaven. Perhaps the most important line in the Bible about reward is found in the book of Revelation where it says the saints will "lay their crowns before the throne."† If there are crowns, they will leave no trace on the heads of the ones who have handed them back to God.

It's all grace.

---

* 2 Corinthians 5:10
† Revelation 4:10

Who Will Be in Heaven?

The Most Important Question in This Book

> Only One has passed that way [into death] and
> lived: the One Who uttered the heart-stoppingly
> incredible claim, "I am the Life."
>
> — Peter Kreeft

Mrs. Rudy Turpin was a bossy, opinionated, racist, judgmental woman who thought she was blessed by God with a good disposition. One day her husband, Claud, was kicked by a cow. Soon the wound began to fester, so off they went to the doctor's office.

As they waited in cramped quarters, Mrs. Turpin spent her time judging everyone in the room. "White-trash" and "ugly" were two classes of people on her list. One young woman in the room, a college student trying to read and growing irritated with Mrs. Turpin's chatter, threw her book at Mrs. Turpin. The book struck her above the eye. Not yet done with her frustration, the young woman attempted to choke Mrs. Turpin.

In the midst of the scuffle, the young woman called Mrs. Turpin an "old wart hog" and urged her to "Go back to hell where you came from." It turns out that the book hit Mrs. Turpin at the very moment she was telling others how thankful she was to Jesus for who she was. She mentioned that she had a little of everything: a good home, a husband, and a good disposition.

Later that evening, after she and Claud had taken an afternoon rest, the words of the young woman began to haunt Mrs. Turpin. In spite of her self-righteousness, having been called a wart hog became a revelation of Mrs. Turpin's real inner world. She had a vision of a swinging bridge reaching from earth to the final Heaven and being used by multitudes of people. The revelation for her was that her entire reality was reversed. The people she had been judging were preceding her own favorite people into Heaven. She also noticed that everyone's "virtues" were being burned up in a way that echoed the folks in the book of Revelation who handed their crowns back to God.

Back at the doctor's office, gospel music was playing over the PA system. Mrs. Turpin silently sang the last line to one song: "And wona these days I know I'll we-eara crown." But her crown of condescending virtues—her church attendance and kindnesses—would be burned away in the purging grace of God's clear vision of who she really was. The young woman who threw a book at Mrs. Turpin was named Mary Grace, and just such a moment of grace typifies the short stories of Flannery O'Connor.[1]

She called this story, one of her last, "Revelation," for that is what it was to Mrs. Turpin. The old woman thought she deserved Heaven only to realize no one did, and it was revealed to her that the bridge to Heaven was filled with surprising revelations. Including who would be there and in what order.

THE BIG QUESTION

Mrs. Turpin was confronted with answers to our question: Who will be in Heaven? Here are typical answers to that question:

- Everyone. The universalist answer.
- People like me. The egocentric answer.
- Most but not all. The good-people-get-in answer.
- People who believe exactly what I believe. The creedal answer.
- People who go to my kind of church. The church answer.
- People who have been baptized. The sacramental answer.

- People who have accepted Christ personally. The decision answer.

And there are other answers:

- We don't know. The agnostic answer.
- It's all speculation anyway. The cynical answer.
- It doesn't matter; what matters is now. The heaven-is-now answer.
- I'll give you some names. The uberconfident answer.
- God could never send people to hell. The God-is-love answer.
- I'm sure your loved one will be. The comforting answer.
- Those who do good. The moralism answer.
- Those who have a good disposition. The character answer.

The question, Who will be in Heaven? necessitates a follow-up question every time: What do we have to do to get into Heaven? Let's look at the first question.

WHO WILL BE IN HEAVEN?

As we look at the answer to this question, it will help if we begin by thinking of a gargantuan Heaven for a gargantuan population. I wonder if our view of Heaven is expansive enough, big enough, or grand enough for it to deserve to be called "Heaven." Here is an example. We find in the book of Revelation a description of the *gargantuan size* of the New Jerusalem. But because so many Bible translations use the word "stadia" instead of our measurement (miles), readers miss out on what has to be one of the great claims about the final Heaven. Here is what the Bible says:

> The angel who talked with me had a measuring rod of gold to measure the city, its gates and its walls. The city was laid out like a square, as long as it was wide. He measured the city with the rod and found it to be 12,000 stadia in length, and as wide and high as it is long.*

Just how big is twelve thousand stadia? First Century readers all broke out with some LOLs and thigh-slapping joy when they heard about the size of this cubed city.

---

* Revelation 21:15–16

It measures 1,500 miles squared. Draw a line from the far coastal corner of the Pacific Northwest to the south, down the US border beyond California into the ocean to a point near Mexico. Then draw a line eastward from that point to near New Orleans. Then continue with a line northward from the spot in Louisiana up to the Canadian border above Wisconsin and back to the starting point in the far Pacific Northwest. That is the footprint, the ground area, covered by the New Jerusalem.

But to get the full dimensions, create a cube based on the foundational dimensions. Go up into space the same distance all the way around those four corners. Now, finally, you have the size of the New Jerusalem. That's 2.25 million square miles. One person computed this to mean the New Jerusalem could house more than 100 billion people! This is no holy huddle for a few saintly folks, friends; this is the Grandpappy of Grand Cities. Surely we are not meant to spend our time computing just how many people will be in Heaven, but one thing we are to hear when we read this text is quite clear: *Heaven is an expanse so high and so wide and so deep that we cannot comprehend its spaciousness.*

Still, people who are drawn to computations have been trying to determine just who gets in and who doesn't. One early American, Joseph Bellamy, had the gall to calculate that only one in every seventeen thousand would enter the gates of Heaven,[2] while not a few well-known theologians and evangelical leaders have been more than generous to say they hope or believe that many (if not the majority of) humans will end up on God's side.[3]

The answer, then, to our first question is "numberless" or "millions and millions and millions." Now, on to the second question: What do we have to do to gain admission to the final Heaven?

WHAT MUST WE DO TO GET INTO HEAVEN?

Too many of us focus on what *we have to do* in order to enter Heaven. The answers are legion. Some say you have to pray the Sinner's Prayer, while others question the prayer itself but think you have to make a genuinely conscious decision. Yet others want to focus on things other than saying a prayer: you must follow Jesus, pursue justice, feed the poor, shelter the homeless, love God, love others, be a good person, develop your inner character by forming good habits, or live as a disciple of Jesus. All of these answers focus on *what we have to do,* and each of them is good and straight out of the Bible. But, we ask, Aren't these answers variations of the general idea of being good? How is this to-do list different in principle from other religions and other faiths and other philosophies?

Here is an ancient Chinese list of what to do if you want to travel the journey into bliss:

The Way can only be received, it cannot be given.

Small, it has no content; great, it has no bounds.

Keep your soul from confusion, and it will come naturally.

Unify the essences and control the spirit; preserve them inside you in
    the midnight hour.

Await it in emptiness, before even Inaction.

All other things proceed from this: this is the Door of Power.[4]

Is this not just an Eastern way of saying more or less the same thing as being good, getting centered, or focusing on God? What makes the Christian faith different?

We discussed earlier the shift back and forth from a theocentric to a kingdom-centric view of Heaven. The former view holds that it's all about God; the latter argues that it's more about perfecting society. In sketching those views of Heaven we might also have observed in that earlier section in the book how these views end up focusing on *what we have to do to get into Heaven.* Everyone seems to have a slightly different answer, and it can be extraordinarily confusing . . .

. . . until we get focused on Jesus!

When I'm asked the question, Who will be in Heaven? my answer is simple: Jesus. I could stop right there because that's how the Bible answers the question. Jesus is the One who lived and died *and was raised into the presence of God and who will be the center of the kingdom forever and ever.* We have to begin to answer the big question with this simple claim: Jesus is in Heaven. But, of course, this leads to the biggest question, the one about Jesus being the only way in. And that belief raises the common objection that it's bigotry to think only Christians go to Heaven.

Again, Peter Kreeft gets it right: "If 'One Way' is bigotry, then it is Jesus Who is the bigot."[5]

You may reply that it's fine to say Jesus is in Heaven, but what about the rest of us? We want to know if *we* are going to Heaven too. The second answer to the question, Who will be in Heaven? is those who are in Christ. I say this because, once again, it was Jesus who cracked through the doom of death and it was Jesus who was raised from the dead and clothed with a glorious body fit for Heaven. It all begins with Jesus, and Jesus promised his followers that he was going to prepare a place for them so they could dwell forever with him.* Heaven is for Jesus and his people.

Max Lucado, in his book about Heaven called *Beyond Heaven's Door*, points us to a memorable truth: that we will be clothed in Christ.[6] In the book of Revelation everyone is wearing white. The victors "will . . . be dressed in white," the twenty-four elders are "dressed in white," and the angels are "dressed in fine linen, white and clean."† Everyone is dressed in white except Jesus. Near the end of the book we are told what Jesus was wearing: "He is dressed in a robe dipped in blood."‡ Blood signifies Jesus's victory over death. Jesus entered into the robe of death, wrestled it to the ground, and suffocated death by his resurrection so we could wear the unbloodied robe of eternal life.

This simple way of answering the question starts with Jesus. It also chases away the confusion and creates breathing space for each of us. All this talk about who goes to Heaven and the tendency to create lists of dos and don'ts and what we have to believe to get into Heaven fail to focus enough on Jesus. Every time we shift the focus away from Jesus, we concentrate on what we have to do to get into Heaven. The focus at that point turns to us. Instead of focusing on *ourselves* and what it takes for *us* and what *we* have to do to get into Heaven, let's focus on *Jesus*.

The question we need to ask is, Are you in Christ? This means that the answer to the question, What do we have to do to get into Heaven? is a big loud . . . nothing! Nothing! Jesus has paved the way, and we simply have to look to him, turn to him, believe in him, and let his life, death, and resurrection be our life, death, and resurrection.

---

* John 14:1–4
† Revelation 3:5; 4:4; 19:14
‡ Revelation 19:13

Of course, this discussion would not be complete without yet another question: Does this mean that Heaven is for Christians alone? Again, we return (with Peter Kreeft) to Jesus. Wasn't it Jesus who said (in John 15:5) that "apart from me you can do nothing"? Yes. Kreeft now pushes back against those who wonder about the sanity of Jesus:

> Dare we pat Him on the head and say, in our superior way, "There, there, now; we know you have to exaggerate a bit to put the fear of God into the uneducated peasants of your unfortunate, benighted era. But we know better. We are The People, and wisdom will die with us. . . . We know there *must* be other ways. Everyone says so. How dare we put all our eggs in one basket— your basket—as you demand? It's not a reasonable investment."
>
> No. It is not. One does not get to Heaven by making reasonable investments. . . . One does not fall in love by making reasonable investments. One falls in love by giving one's all. That is what He demands. Love will not settle for anything less.

And he takes us to the right place, Kreeft does, by standing in the empty tomb looking out:

> Only One has passed that way [into death] and lived: the One Who uttered the heart-stoppingly incredible claim, "I am the Life."[7]

So we ask one last time, Who will be in Heaven? The answer is *Jesus and those who are in him.*

19

Is God Fair?

The Haunting Worry About the God of Heaven

How could an all-loving, all-powerful God allow so much
suffering on earth and *then* send so many suffering souls to
hell to experience eternal damnation?

— The Question so many are asking

One of the most potent moments in my entire teaching career was a one-minute
comment by a student in my office after class. The topic of the course was
Hell and Universalism, and the course was offered to advanced students in Bible and
theology. The Internet was abuzz with discussions about the topic because a few
Christian leaders had come out against the traditional viewpoint of the church. So
the class was of deep interest to our students.

After day two in class, a student came into my office and shared her thoughts
with me. I will summarize what she said in three statements:

*"I don't believe in the traditional view of the church about Heaven being only
for Christians."*

*"Why? Because the man I work for is a Jew who doesn't believe in Jesus but who
is the loving-est person I have ever met."*

"If the God of the Bible sends my boss to hell, then I can't believe that God is just."

I told her that I wondered if the church's traditional beliefs were that simple. Then I encouraged her that if she kept her mind open as we studied the topic, she would hear a more complex and believable account of what the Bible teaches.

Don't allow the brevity of this chapter to lead you to think that the topic lacks weight or importance. The question we now turn to is asked as frequently, if not more frequently, than any question having to do with Heaven. In fact, this one question serves several purposes. For one, it is a touchstone for the unconvinced:

- How could an all-loving, all-powerful God allow so much suffering on earth and *then* send so many suffering souls to hell to experience eternal damnation?

- Why would a loving God arbitrarily decide to send multiplied hundreds of millions of Hindus, Buddhists, Taoists, Shintoists, Muslims, Jews, animists (and all people who lived before 40 CE) to hell to endure eternal suffering just because they were born into the wrong culture or in the wrong epoch?

- How could a loving God decide in advance that there is one, and only one, path to Heaven, and that the path goes through Jesus, when we all know that the lion's share of the earth's human population past, present, and future never had a chance to even hear the name of Jesus?

Such questions are not a smoke screen designed to throw beginning evangelists off track. For the most part they are questions arising from honest reflection on a thorny issue. When we talk about Heaven, and that's just what we're doing, what are we to say about all the non-Westerners throughout history (the vast majority of the human population) who lived entire lives, generation following generation, without any Christian influence or gospel message being present in their culture or locale?

It's a fair question.

FOUR IMPORTANT POINTS, PLUS GOD'S LOVE AND GOODNESS

If we call up a few philosophers and invite them to a coffee shop and ask them the question, "Is God fair when it comes to a person's entering heaven through Christ alone?" the day could get very long very fast. So instead of inviting them to this little table for that conversation, I want to summarize a philosopher's view that makes the most sense to me. His name is Jerry Walls, and in his splendid academic book on heaven, he addresses this question. Here is a summary of his arguments:[1]

First, on the basis of the Bible's general depiction of God—the God of love, the God of mercy, the God of justice, the God of holiness—I believe we need to begin to answer this question by affirming that God is perfectly and eternally good.

Second, this perfectly good God loves all human beings equally. God doesn't love Europeans or Americans any more than God loves Asians or Africans, though some have a better shot at hearing the gospel than others.

Third, this good God of love has chosen to redeem humans in and through a single Person, his Son Jesus. The Christian faith stands or falls right here for just one reason. The *Christian belief in Heaven depends on the fact that God—this good God of love—raised this Jesus from the dead and accepted that same Jesus into the throne room of God.*

Fourth, and now we come to the crucial point that, to my way of thinking, makes the most sense of the Bible and the reality in which we all live: this good God of love, *to be good and to be loving of all people equally,* gives to each person *a full and fair opportunity* to know God and to respond to God's love in Christ. I cannot see how God can be good and loving and not make it possible for each person to respond to his love.

We don't know how God makes these opportunities possible for each person in history—past, present, and future. But we can trust the God of promise to accomplish what he wants to do because this God is good and this God is loving.

How does God work things out so that everyone gets an opportunity to know and accept Christ? Walls mentions four options. It gets a bit speculative at this point, so we need to keep the big picture in mind. That big picture, regardless of which of the four options resonate with you, is that God is good, God is love, God redeems in Christ, and God grants to each person a fair opportunity to respond to his love. Jerry Walls explores four possible ways God gives everyone an opportunity, but he chooses to focus on the problem of those who do not *seem* to get an opportunity in this life.

Some will have an opportunity:

- At the moment of death.
- Or God knows on the basis of his infinite knowledge, how each person would have responded had each person been given a full and fair opportunity, and God judges on this basis.
- Or after death in the postmortem state, God gives persons a full and fair opportunity.
- But probably the most common view is that God will judge each person on the "light" he or she has received in this life but that there are no opportunities from the moment of death on.

I confess that I am not confident the Bible allows us to answer this question with absolute confidence. I believe God is good, God is fair, God redeems in Christ, and God is loving. While I believe that God will give each person a full and fair opportunity, I don't know how God makes that happen. A case can be made for each view, and that is where we might have to let the matter rest; we don't know, but we can be confident in the God of promise who raised Jesus from the dead for us.

20

Will There Be Families?

Rethinking What the Bible Says

When I myself come to cross that boundary that she has
crossed, I think I shall find her hand and hear her voice first
of all. Perhaps by the old lily pond at Glenmerle.

— Sheldon Vanauken

I was told as a child that when we get to Heaven there will be no families, which for
children is nearly always a bit frightening. Later, when I was a teenager, the doctrine of no-parents-in-Heaven sounded like a future that could not come soon
enough. But as an adult, as a husband, as a father, and as a grandfather, I have absolutely no desire to be in a Heaven that erases my memories of family or that eliminates from my life those I most love. It is hard to imagine the new Heavens and the
new earth as being full of joy if I won't recognize my family.

But many in the history of the church believe we will not be reunited as families
in heaven. Randy Alcorn expressed the no-families-in-Heaven viewpoint when he
wrote, "Heaven won't be without families but will be one big family, in which all family members are friends and all friends are family members."[1] Alcorn's view, which
excludes marital unions in Heaven, is quite common among Christians. For instance,
Arthur Roberts has "concluded that the most ecstatic orgasm ever experienced in a

love-caressed marriage won't hold a candle to what touch and taste and smell and sight and sound will bring to 'children of the resurrection,' to persons sanctified and glorified by the Holy Spirit."[2] And James Garlow and Keith Wall wrote, "In heaven you will know oneness with your spouse beyond what you could ever know on this earth."[3] That word "beyond" means it will not be physical as it is now.

But—and this shouldn't surprise anyone who knows how many different ideas there are about Heaven—many disagree with the no-families-in-Heaven and no-marriages-in-Heaven notions, and even the no-sex-in-Heaven view. I will suggest that there is only one text in the Bible that raises this topic, and while there is a very strong conventional understanding (represented above), there are some good reasons to rethink if the one biblical text is saying what church tradition has believed.

REUNION IN HEAVEN WITH FRIENDS

A good starting point in this complex discussion is belief in reunion with friends after earthly death. Sheldon Vanauken put on paper the best-told love story of the twentieth century, recording the depth of commitment he and his wife, Davy, had for one another. Their love was rooted in two principles, one they called the Shining Barrier, which was a line that separated them from the whole world, and the second principle was a commitment to share everything with each other.[4]

It so happens that in the lives of many lovers, one of them takes a new path but the other does not. One becomes a Christian and the other does not; one wants to enter into ministry when the other resists such a call; one feels compelled to unite with one church denomination while the other finds no compelling reason. Davy's curiosity gave way to the Christian faith while Sheldon lagged, even though C. S. Lewis, who became a friend to both while they were in Oxford, told him, "The Holy Spirit is after you. I doubt if you'll get away!" As is also often the case, one finds the grace to catch up with the other, which happened to Sheldon Vanauken as their love story took surprising turns and gentle twists while they kept their original two commitments.

At their last meeting, Lewis said to Sheldon, "I shan't say goodbye. We'll meet again." Then, as Sheldon tells that story, Lewis crossed the street, looked back to him, and announced before the world that "Christians NEVER say goodbye!"[5]

Here we encounter a glimmer of what many Christians genuinely believe: in Heaven we shall meet again, in Heaven we shall find one another. This hope sustains so many who endure the sudden and early deaths of those they love most, as was the case with Sheldon and Davy.

REUNION IN HEAVEN WITH FAMILY AND SPOUSES

What seems at the moment to be a normal kind of illness—perhaps a cold or a sneeze or a funny pain in the lower back—may become a dreaded or deadly diagnosis, which is what happened to Davy when she caught a virus. Doctors often enough convey this information privately to those the patient loves, and such happened with Sheldon when he was told she had "maybe six months" to survive. In the quiet of intimate conversations with one another, loved ones often begin to talk about their reunion in Heaven—offering words that express both adoring love and confident hope.

"Dearling," Sheldon said to her, "this—this illness—is maybe going to mean our parting..." And I love how Sheldon ended that sentence: "for awhile." Words like this turn into embraces and tears and hope as lovers face a future of separation.

Hope of reunion—nay, confidence in reunion after deaths—forms the core of how we console one another in death. The reason for this is not shallow thinking but one that springs eternal from Jesus's reunion with his followers after his resurrection and from the joyful scenes in the book of Revelation. There is a "back with one another" dimension to all Christian belief in Heaven.

Once again, reunion is the theme for Sheldon: "If there's anything I'm sure of, it is that heaven is...for us, Glenmerle." In these moments many reflect, as did this ideal loving couple, that they could die together and that especially the time will be short between parting and reunion. Sheldon's famous words continue to this day to stir those who love another as they did:

> When I myself come to cross that boundary that she has crossed, I think I shall find her hand and hear her voice first of all. Perhaps by the old lily pond at Glenmerle. [6]

Is this wishful hoping? Are C. S. Lewis and Sheldon and Davy Vanauken a clique of mistaken friends? Have so many gotten this all wrong? Will we reunite with our loved ones? Will we become family again, a whole, intimate, loving and thriving family? Or, as some would put it, will Heaven be so grand that even their love behind the Shining Barrier will be transcended in a grand communion of the saints?

LET'S LOOK AT THE BIBLE

At the heart of my own argument is the belief that Christians need to form their beliefs about Heaven on the basis of the Bible. They may be curious about what great theologians have taught, they may well know that Dante's *Divine Comedy* and John Bunyan's *Pilgrim's Progress* and C. S. Lewis's *Chronicles of Narnia* have shaped the thinking of more than a few regarding Heaven. But in the end Christians should believe that God has revealed what is most important in the Bible. That does not, however, mean the Bible is absolutely clear on everything we'd like to know. But it does mean we need to begin with the Bible. This discussion about reunions and friends and families and marriages in Heaven is rooted in three passages in the Bible.

#1: Mark 3:31–35

Some feel that Jesus's brusque words to his mother indicate the earthly understanding of family already was fading into the eternal fellowship of Heaven. It is true that Jesus downplays his natural family when someone approached with the news that his mother and siblings were at the door. Here is how Mark records the event. Someone informs Jesus that "your mother and brothers are outside looking for you." Jesus's potent and family-checking response? "Who are my mother and my brothers?" Jesus said this because he wanted those around him to see the deeper connection. Looking at his disciples, Jesus said: "Here are my mother and my brothers! Whoever does God's will is my brother and sister and mother."* But this text does not say anything about the identity and connections of earthly families once family members arrive in Heaven. What it does say is that Heaven is for those who are connected to Jesus. However, when family members are connected to Jesus . . . well, it doesn't say they

---

* Mark 3:31–35; see also Matthew 12:46–50 and Luke 8:19–21

will or will not be reunited. This text is of little to no use in our question about the reuniting of families and spouses in Heaven.

#2: John 2:1–11

In another passage Jesus had a similar family-checking experience. He was at a wedding in Cana when his mother informed him they had run out of wine, to which Jesus said, "Woman, why do you involve me?"* Yes, these words serve to remind even his mother that his priorities transcend her and his allegiances are higher than to family. But these words of Jesus are no more than a stiff reminder that our union with Christ is deeper than family unions. This text puts families in their place under God but says nothing about reunion with families and spouses in Heaven. Everything hinges on the third passage.

#3: Mark 12:18–27

I have reformatted this passage in Mark's gospel slightly, and I ask you to read this text carefully enough to see what it actually says to avoid reading into it what it *does not* say.†

The Law

> Then the Sadducees, who say there is no resurrection, came to him with a question. "Teacher," they said, "Moses wrote for us that if a man's brother dies and leaves a wife but no children, the man must marry the widow and raise up offspring for his brother."

A Scenario Creates a Problem for the Law

> "Now there were seven brothers. The first one married and died without leaving any children. The second one married the widow, but he also died, leaving no child. It was the same with the third. In fact, none of the seven left any children. Last of all, the woman died too."

---

* John 2:4
† Mark 12:18–27; see also Matthew 22:23–33 and Luke 20:27–40

The Question for Jesus

"At the resurrection whose wife will she be, since the seven were married to her?"

Jesus replied,

(1) "Are you not in error because you do not know the Scriptures or the power of God?

(2) "When the dead rise, they will neither marry nor be given in marriage; they will be like the angels in heaven.

(3) "Now about the dead rising—have you not read in the Book of Moses, in the account of the burning bush, how God said to him, 'I am the God of Abraham, the God of Isaac, and the God of Jacob'? He is not the God of the dead, but of the living.

(4) "You are badly mistaken!"

Jesus lived in a world where not all of the Jewish leaders even believed in a resurrection. The major political players in Jerusalem, the Sadducees, believed only in the first five books of our Old Testament (the Pentateuch, or the Torah), and since there was no evidence of resurrection in the Torah, they did not believe in a resurrection. The Pharisees, who embraced the prophets and tradition, believed in resurrection after death. So did Jesus, and that put Jesus smack-dab in the middle of a theological controversy between the Pharisees and Sadducees—not unlike getting caught between Baptists and Catholics on what to believe about the Lord's Supper.

Jesus always had a way of torching the cards on the table when they stuck him in the middle of their debates, and that's how we have to read this passage. To prove their point, the Sadducees had an argument that can be reduced to this:[7]

1. We are to obey God's Law eternally.
2. If the woman in question is married in heaven, she will have to be married to seven men at once, and polygamy is against the Law, or
3. She will have to divorce six men, which also is against the Law.

Therefore, there is no resurrection.

#boom #SadduceesWin! #PhariseesLose!

This logic attempts to prove that either there is no resurrection, or that God condones either polygamy (one woman, seven men, poor woman!) or divorce in the resurrection life. Therefore, the Pharisees are wrong. So the Sadducees turn to Jesus and ask, "What do you think, Jesus? Which team are you on?"

Jesus beat the Sadducees at their own game when he quoted from the Torah. In quoting from Exodus 3,* Jesus affirmed the resurrection, then spoke about what humans will be like in Heaven. "When the dead rise," he said (disagreeing with the Sadducees), "they will neither marry nor be given in marriage; they will be like the angels in heaven."

Now to the question: Does Jesus here say there will be no families or marriage in Heaven? I'm going to suggest that a careful look leads to "No, that is not what he was getting at."

NO MARRIAGE IN HEAVEN?

Once again, the traditional view can be seen in what Augustine taught: "All special attachments [marriage, family, friendships] will be absorbed into one comprehensive and undifferentiated community of love."[8] An additional interpretation emboldens this traditional view: When Jesus mentioned that we will be "like the angels," he meant *unmarried* and probably without gender. This interpretation, I will suggest, goes far beyond what Jesus actually said in his response to the Sadducees.

MARRIAGE IN HEAVEN?

Here is my boldest and most complex claim: what Jesus said is *not* that there won't be marital life in Heaven. He could have said that quite easily, making the statement straight out, but he didn't. He could have said, "In heaven there will be no marriages and families." Instead, he said, "They will neither marry nor be given in marriage." That statement by Jesus does not say people who are now married won't remain in a married state in Heaven. It says only that there *will be no new marriages*. Again,

---

* See Exodus 3:6, quoted in Mark 12:26

neither does it speak a word about sex or procreation or pleasure; this text only says there will be no new marriages.

I have to quote his words and set them off so they will stand out:

"They will neither marry nor be given in marriage."

The first part—"will neither marry"—is a reference to a groom who marries, and the second—"be given in marriage"—points to a bride being given away in marriage. Look at it again. The text does not say "no families" or "no marriages." It says there will be *no weddings or new marriages* in Heaven.

Why? Because we will be like the angels. And what does that mean? In the traditional view this means "Angels don't have a gender, we'll be like the angels, and therefore there will be no marriage or families in heaven." Once again, what does this text actually say? The best way to look at this is to observe the three places the saying is found in the Gospels:

Mark 12:25: "They will be like the angels in heaven."
Matthew 22:30: "They will be like the angels in heaven."

Those two texts say the same thing, but notice Luke clarifies:

Luke 20:36: "They can no longer die; *for they are like the angels.*"

Anyone reading the Bible can see the difference here. Being "like the angels" does not mean being single or without gender. It means never *dying.* Jesus was saying the major reason for marriage is to procreate in order to continue one's seed or heritage. But Heaven people are eternal, so one will not need to procreate in order to continue the family line.

In the end, then, Jesus is not talking about families in Heaven but about *a very common Jewish problem: if a man dies without children, how will his seed continue?* The Jewish answer was that his brother is to create offspring in his place. Jesus says there will be no need to continue a man's line in Heaven since everyone will live eternally. He also said that God's transformative power is great enough to make this all good and perfect for all concerned. Remember, however, it all is predicated on one assumption: *the resurrection itself.* The stumbling block for the Sadducees was the only possible solution for Jesus!

Three texts then have been used to teach that there will be no families in Heaven. The first two have nothing to do with that topic, and the third, at least as I read it, joins them in having nothing to do with the topic. *If these texts do not suggest there is no marriage or family life in heaven, no text in the Bible does. We are then to presume that in Heaven our families and marriages will be intact.* Now you may well ask the question the Sadducees asked! But, what about . . . ? I appeal to God's transformative power to create anew in the final Heaven, and it will *at least* be like our marriages and families now *and so much more.*

If we learn to think biblically about questions like this, we must always think about it through the reality of the resurrection of Jesus. As the resurrected body was both like and more than Jesus's earthly body, so our relationships—friends, family, marriage—will be both like and more than they are now.

WHAT WILL IT BE LIKE TO BE MARRIED AND HAVE FAMILIES IN HEAVEN?

If we are married in Heaven, then it follows that we will live a normal family life— perhaps like happy holiday gatherings with adult children and more adult children . . . again, I'm guessing. But it will be *at least that.*

This much is certain: Jesus's words do not explicitly say there will be no marriages, but instead that there'll be no *new* marriages. If that is the case, then there are marriages, and if there are marriages, there are families . . . and that fires the imagination, which is just about what everything in the Bible is designed to do when it comes to our wondering what the kingdom of God will be like. C. S. Lewis will be reunited with Joy and with Sheldon and Davy Vanauken because, it is true, Christians never say good-bye to one another. They will grow as families and best friends forever into more than they could ever imagine.

What About Children Who Die?

Faith's Search for Wisdom

> We have no alternative other than to leave the
> matter in the hands of a God we have come to
> trust as fully just and fully loving.
>
> — Graham Twelftree

Many readers of this book will be from a Western world saturated and pro-
tected by the marvels of modern medicine and scientific advancements. Not
least in these advancements is the survival rate of infants. Approximately 994 out of
one thousand infants in the United States will survive until their first birthday.[1]
(Japan is at almost 998, Sweden is at almost 997, Germany is at 994, with the tragic
reality of Afghanistan having a survival of only about 848.)[2]

We can make this question more dense by asking about children who are
aborted. What about Heaven for them? A friend of mine, Karen Spears Zacharias,
has told of her choice as a teenager to have an abortion.[3] In a conversation with her
about Heaven and abortion, she wrote me this:

When my own children—the four I have now—reached the ages of four-
teen, twelve, and ten, Tim and I sat them down and told them about my

abortion. I wanted them to hear the story from me. They were shocked, of course. Cried a bunch. As did I. I asked their forgiveness, since, after all, this was a half-sibling of theirs.

Later that afternoon, as I was loading laundry in the washing machine, Ashley and Shelby came to me. Ashley handed me a sheet of paper.

"We came up with a name for our baby," Shelby said.

They had taken a letter from each of our names and created a name for the unborn child:

Kasey.

Oh, how I wept as those girls handed me that! And I've wept several times since.

So, a long answer to your question, Scot. I believe the day will come when I will meet the child named Kasey. I believe that as well about babies that are miscarried or stillborn.

Whether we give that baby a name or not, God has given that child a soul.[4]

What will happen to those whose life is ended before it has a chance to begin?

Join me in thinking about this: If God is good and God is loving and God is fair and just, what happens to babies who die before they have an opportunity to hear about God's grace or who are snatched from life itself? As we discovered in the previous chapter, some of the most important questions and their truths about Heaven are not plainly spelled out in the Bible. Such is the case as we consider the eternal state of infants and children who die prematurely. The lack of biblical clarity and detail in response to this question has not discouraged the formulation of a number of confident-sounding answers. Diverse theological streams have come up with their own hard-and-fast positions, as we will soon see. However, as with many doctrinal and theological statements, Christian arguments can easily miss the bigger, foundational ideas—a central focus of this book—that should guide us.

As we look at the question regarding the eternal destination of infants and children who die young, let's not lose sight of God. God's nature/God's character does not change. And while Christian traditions multiply with the subdividing of the church, we need to seek answers that go beyond theological allegiances and loyalties to doctrinal convictions that serve to identify your chosen group. (Remember the Sadducees and Pharisees, who differed on the resurrection in the time of Jesus.) Amid ongoing debate and evolving viewpoints, God is still God. As we seek an answer to the question "What about children who die?" let's not lose sight of God. God is love. God is good. God is just.

WILL ALL INFANTS AND CHILDREN WHO DIE YOUNG BE IN HEAVEN?

So what does happen to infants and young children, who are by nature incapable of embracing Christ, if they die before they are old enough to be responsible before God? There are four basic options:

1. All will be in Heaven (the generous view).
2. All will go to hell (the rigorous view).
3. Some will be in Heaven (the restrictive view), often based on being baptized as children, being the children of Christians, or being children who are themselves elect or those whom God knows would have believed had they lived longer on earth.
4. All will enter into a sphere around Heaven but will not experience Heaven's blessedness (the almost-but-not-quite view, sometimes called *limbo*).

The death of children brings to the surface what one believes about God, what one believes about Heaven, and what one believes about entry into Heaven. It returns us to the previous question about whether God is fair.

Not long ago I read the story of the very scrupulous Sarah Osborn, an early American Puritan Christian woman who faced more than her fair share of suffering. Her eleven-year-old son, Samuel, in her judgment was not a true believer. When he was in the throes of death, he became for his mother a source of intense reflection.

In her diary she observed that Samuel was "much swelled with a dropsy [edema, or swelling of the tissues], and pined to a mere skeleton with the jaundice, scurvy, and consumption." In her aching desire to know the eternal state of her son, Sarah Osborn wrote out her thoughts. As one intimately attuned both to her son and to his spiritual condition, she knew "there had been no passionate confessions of sinfulness, no tears of repentance, no overpowering joy." Her very strict Calvinism pushed forward the idea that what mattered was whether her son was one of the elect, but "she was terrified that he might go to hell." As Samuel lay dying, Sarah "sat by his side reading the book [a book shaped to warn sinners of hell and promise them God's Heaven] aloud, praying for some small sign of conversion." None appeared. As she wrote it up later, "In his dying moments, I had an awful sense of his deplorable condition."

Convinced that Samuel had experienced no genuine conversion, Sarah began to make sense of her nightmare by seeing God's hand of discipline. As her biographer, Catherine Brekus, described it, "She claimed that God had taken her son for two reasons: to make her more dependent on his divine grace and to show other Christians how to accept their afflictions without 'murmuring.'" But she went further: "*This* was Sarah's sin: she had loved her son even more than God. Because she had worshiped Samuel as an idol, God had taken him away. His death was her fault."[5] It's all here: her view of God's stern love was discriminatory, her view of Heaven was that it was only for the holy converted, and her view of how to get there shaped her every move.

Yet, most who read this today come away pondering how God could send children — Samuel was hardly an adult and capable of a fully rational decision — to hell. In fact, many today would find Sarah's view of her son's soul intolerable, and her view of God just as intolerable (if not cruel). How should we think about this? Does the Bible tell us?[6]

Not explicitly, so we are driven to think about this kind of topic on the basis of sound biblical reasoning in light of the big ideas about God's Heaven Promise. It is worth observing that many theologians, including well-known names like Charles Hodge, B. B. Warfield, John Stott, and Billy Graham, have recorded their belief that infants who die will be in Heaven, but perhaps even the majority of humans will be there too.

I have landed on three observations about God:

- God is love.
- God is good.
- God is just.

These three observations have led me to two conclusions:

- Because God is loving, good, and just, God cannot send children into eternal darkness.
- Because God is loving, good, and just, God will send those who die in infancy or prior to their maturity into what is most right for such persons.

Graham Twelftree expressed it perfectly for those who want to think through these issues on the basis of what the Bible teaches: "We have no alternative other than to leave the matter in the hands of a God we have come to trust as fully just and totally loving."[7] So when someone asks me where an infant or a child is after a premature death, I answer with this: "In the hands of our good God." I am confident in the God who promises Heaven.

What About Cremation?

Wisdom That Respects God's World

For dust you are and to dust you will return.

—The Bible

Cremation is becoming more and more common. In fact, some 1.2 million Americans are cremated every year. Several trends are driving the increase in numbers, and among the most important are space and finances. As funerals become more expensive, families seek more financially reasonable approaches to observing the death of a loved one. Furthermore, cemeteries consume space, and as available space in many regions is decreasing, cremation is a simple way to save space. There also are spiritual or mystical reasons for preferring cremation, such as scattering ashes to the winds or into the ocean or over a favored part of the world. Still others feel that funerals are an objectionable wallowing in mourning or an unnecessary consumption of the time of others.

While cremation grows in popularity, some are objecting based on theological grounds. One argument is straightforward: "They didn't cremate in the Bible so we shouldn't cremate today." Others believe that the body traps the soul, and the sooner we can get rid of the body the better, so cremation is the quickest route to total liberation. But for such persons, cremation also seems to reflect a devaluing of the body itself, and the body, as the temple of the Holy Spirit, is highly valued in the Bible.

Far more important is this: the Bible does not teach that the soul is trapped by the body. (In fact, that is an ancient Greek but not biblical theory.) Jesus's resurrected body was the transformation of his earthly body, not the eradication or annihilation of that body. The same is true for us. So we should take a closer look at the reason for cremation to see if it squares up to how the Bible values body and soul.

There is a solidly biblical way to look at cremation as a reasonable and thoroughly acceptable method of disposing of the body. The first of two points is this: we were made from dust, and after death we return to our dustiness. I like how the Bible talks about death as our returning to dust, but I like this language because I know dust isn't the last word:

> By the sweat of your brow
>   you will eat your food
> until you return to the ground,
>   since from it you were taken;
> *for dust you are*
>   *and to dust you will return.*

> You turn people back to dust,
>   saying, *"Return to dust, you mortals."*

> When you hide your face,
>   they are terrified;
> *when you take away their breath,*
>   *they die and return to the dust.*
> *. . . and the dust returns to the ground it came from,*
>   *and the spirit returns to God who gave it.*

---

* Genesis 3:19; Psalm 90:3; Psalm 104:29; and Ecclesiastes 12:7.

Cremation, in other words, simply *speeds up our inevitable return to dust,* from which dust God will remake us into our resurrection bodies designed for the final Heaven.

In the *Book of Common Prayer,* which is used by Anglicans throughout the world, we read these important words for funerals:

> In sure and certain hope of the resurrection to eternal life through our Lord Jesus Christ, we commend to Almighty God our brother/sister. And we commit his body to the ground, earth to earth, ashes to ashes, dust to dust. The Lord bless him and keep him, the Lord make his face to shine upon him and be gracious unto him, the Lord lift up his countenance upon him and give him peace. Amen.[1]

That language of returning to dust applies whether we have an ordinary disposal in a cheap wooden box, in a tragic burial at sea, in a location no one ever discovers, in an expensive gold-plated casket, or in the fires of cremation.

What matters is the resurrection of Jesus and our participation in his resurrection. As Billy Graham once said, "The body is annihilated just as completely in the grave as it is in cremation. . . . Cremation is therefore no hindrance to the resurrection."[2]

What About Purgatory?

A Theory That Divides the Church

> It will be revealed with fire, and the fire will test the quality
> of each person's work. If what has been built survives, the
> builder will receive a reward. If it is burned up, the builder
> will suffer loss but yet will be saved—even though only as
> one escaping through the flames.
>
> —The apostle Paul to the Corinthians

Does being reconciled with God and with others in the first hour in Heaven require that we remember fully what happened in the past? Does it mean conscious repentance and reconciliation in the presence of others with God monitoring the moment? Does it mean going through each and every sin and making each and every thing right? Does it mean we have to have our character consciously purified by an eternal review board? And if we answer yes to one or more of these questions, does that mean that the time of reconciliation is a kind of purgatory?

I don't think so, but we do need to give this question serious thought. What also deserves some serious thought is for us to learn just what some traditions in the church have taught about purgatory. Over and over I have heard especially from Protestants and evangelicals that Roman Catholics believe in a second chance and they equate that second chance with purgatory. I have heard nearly the same at times from (uninformed) Roman Catholics. So, before we can evaluate the biblical basis for such a view, we must understand just what this term *purgatory* means.

Purgatory refers to a state or period between death and the final Heaven where, it is alleged by some theologians and ministers, those who are in Christ will be purged of their sins.[1] Why do they need to be purged? These are the two reasons given: (1) to stand in God's presence, we must be made worthy of that presence; and (2) no one dies in a state of perfection. Therefore, something has to happen to make someone worthy of God's presence. At this point Protestants and Catholics take different paths. The Protestants agree with the two points but believe *God in his grace will instantaneously make humans fit for God's presence by an act of glorification.* Roman Catholics, emphasizing more a belief in human will, believe *humans will cooperate with God as God makes that person fit for that glorious presence.* Hence, either one believes in glorification by a sudden act of God's grace, or one believes in purgatory.

For those who want biblical evidence for purgatory, there are two possible texts to examine. One of those is found in what we commonly call the Old Testament *Apocrypha,* which is not printed as part of the Bible by Protestants. So we begin there even though that text is not considered authoritative for Protestants.*

In the second-century-BC battles to regain control of Jerusalem, Judah Maccabeus led his armies into a number of battles. One was waged against a leader named Gorgias in a region called Idumaea. In that battle, some of Judah's men died. What happened next is not like anything else found in the Old Testament, but by the time of the Maccabees was an evidently common custom. What custom? Praying for the souls of the dead that they might join in the final resurrection.

In collecting the bodies of the fallen to take them home for burial, the military leaders discovered that the fallen were wearing "amulets" or "sacred tokens" that reflected some kind of idolatrous practice. The leaders prayed for these men in the hope that God would forgive their sins. What can we learn from this? First, that some Jewish leaders believed in prayer for the already dead in the hope that their

---

* 2 Maccabees 12:32–45

prayers would lead to the forgiveness of sins committed by others. Second, that they believed in a resurrection from the dead. While this text does not suggest a belief in purgatory, it does suggest something can happen to the people of God *after death* and *before the resurrection*. Nothing more should be inferred from this text. There is no evidence here for belief in purgatory.

A second text is thought by some to supply a basis for a belief in purgatory. The apostle Paul seems to be saying in 1 Corinthians that either at death or after death the things we have done in our earthly lives will be tested by fire. What survives the test is eternal, and what doesn't survive will be burned with fire. The word "fire" in Greek is *pur* from which the word *purgatory*—burned or perfected by fire—comes.*

Here are Paul's words, but a careful reading of the text shows that works, not people, are being tested (and approved):†

> For no one can lay any foundation other than the one already laid, which is Jesus Christ. If anyone builds on this foundation using gold, silver, costly stones, wood, hay or straw, their work will be shown for what it is, because the Day will bring it to light. *It will be revealed with fire, and the fire will test the quality of each person's work. If what has been built survives, the builder will receive a reward. If it is burned up, the builder will suffer loss but yet will be saved—even though only as one escaping through the flames.*

A significant element of later beliefs about purgatory, namely fire that purges, is clearly present here. But the two most distinctive elements of purgatory, namely, that humans are to work off their sins through repentance under God's disciplinary hands and that all this occurs after death, are wholly absent from Paul's statements. The purging we find in the New Testament describes life in the here and now. I find no biblical basis for purgatory in either of these texts.

In fact, what this text does reveal is that at death (or at the judgment just prior to the final Heaven itself) God judges our works and purges (or sanctifies us and

---

* Latin is similar; purgare means "to purge" or "to make clean."
† 1 Corinthians 3:11–15

glorifies us) from our corruptions so that we will be fit for the presence of God. In the Bible, the fire that purges is an act of God and not something in which we participate.

I must also add that beliefs about purgatory, because they focus so much on *what we do to get ourselves ready for Heaven,* diminish what Christ does for us. Personally, I find no biblical basis for purgatory and find that it contradicts what God does for us and to us by grace.

This at times needs to be said more forcefully: there is a real danger in the doctrine of purgatory in minimizing the completeness of God's work for us in Christ and the importance of God's grace. To use the words of Graham Twelftree, the theory of purgatory seems to "stretch the imagination more than solve the problem."[2]

Will There Be Pets in Heaven?

What God Creates God Perfects

Well, dogs don't have souls, you see. But anything is
possible with God. He will do what is best for us.

— Rich Mouw and his mother

Many of us have or have had pets and have stories to tell about our dog or cat
or turtle or fish or hamster. When I was a boy, I had a black Labrador named
Sam who helped me deliver papers. Actually, he didn't help me because, as a re-
triever, every time I threw a paper, he ran after it and brought it back to me. I had to
learn to trick Sam or walk up to the porch and drop the paper, rather than throw it.
The matter was resolved somehow by a curious development. Sam got far more in-
terested in running off and chasing rabbits and snooping around neighborhoods
than walking with me. His disinterest in what I was doing allowed me once again to
throw papers from sidewalks. Sam, by the instinct that dogs alone somehow develop,
would catch up to me in the last block of my paper route and by then he was worn
out from all his own running. Sam was a good companion for me as a boy. When
we moved and I stopped delivering papers, Sam didn't adjust well—he would start
barking at about 5:00 a.m. because I hadn't come out to take him with me on the
paper route. That lasted about a week. Then neighborly complaints led my parents

to find a more suitable environment for Sam on someone's farm. So Sam and I parted ways.

Many wonder if that separation will end in Heaven. Many wonder this: If God has made the world and saw fit to create a world in which we gain so much joy with pets, won't Heaven *at least* have pets that are even more delightful? For many of us, the answer is an immediate yes!

The Christmas card art called "peaceable kingdom" features a lion lying down with a lamb. And as far as I know, the depiction has not given rise to heated debate over the appropriateness of the characters in the art. I don't mean fights over a lion coexisting willingly with a lamb: that's not the issue. I mean there has been no prolonged uproar over the presence of animals in Heaven. At least when the mammals in question are an unrivaled predator and a lovable source of wool and cutlets.

The same, however, cannot be said for mammals that we readily associate with family life and playing a prominent role in the home. These are dogs and cats, mostly, but also hamsters, gerbils, guinea pigs, rabbits, tropical fish, and blue parakeets. If you read books about Heaven, you know that the presence in eternity—or the exclusion from Heaven—of a favorite family pet can quickly become a source of contention.

Whether in or out, there is no question we are attached to pets. Just look at the photos posted on social media and the videos on YouTube—you know, the spontaneous smartphone footage that charms viewers with a cute household pet doing something brave, amusing, or endearing.

People love pets, and most of us are hoping that we'll all be together in Heaven. But will we?

Do All Dogs Go to Heaven?

Some think pets will be in Heaven, as we saw in the 1989 animated film *All Dogs Go to Heaven*. Rich Mouw was not the only child to have asked his mother if there would be pets in Heaven because, as he tells the story, his own son asked him the same question years later. His response mirrored his mom's response to him years earlier: "Well, dogs don't have souls, you see. But anything is possible with God. He will do what is best for us." Mouw, the veteran theologian, then proceeds to a key question: "Why do we assume that only things with 'souls' will participate in the New Age [Heaven]?"[1]

Maybe we can ask another question: Why stop with pets? What about animals and plant life and all God's creations? Will they all cease in Heaven? I doubt it, or it would be a duller place than what we enjoy now on earth, and Heaven has to be better in order to be Heaven! I agree with Mouw that the prophet Isaiah provides one of the Bible's first glimpses of God's promise of a utopian, final Heaven (as the new Heavens and the new earth), and that we probably ought to let its images sink more deeply into our thinking.

The wolf will live with the lamb,
    the leopard will lie down with the goat,
the calf and the lion and the yearling together;
    and a little child will lead them.
The cow will feed with the bear,
    their young will lie down together,
    and the lion will eat straw like the ox.
The infant will play near the cobra's den,
    the young child will put its hand into the viper's nest.

Mouw's observation on these verses (Isaiah 11:6–8) is worth quoting: "Former predators will live peacefully with their former prey. Little children will have nothing to fear from beasts and snakes."[2] And if the children are not afraid of them, the animals will have to be there for that fear not to be there!

Pets are a featured item on the list of God's good creations, which includes mountains and lakes and rivers and trees and flowers and grasses. Here is one of the big ideas about Heaven: what God makes God perfects, and what God has made for this world will be perfected in the kingdom of God. If we take the body of Jesus as our model, then Heaven is filled with the same things we know and experience here, only at the glorified, eternal level. God will, I suggest, decorate his world with magnificent trees and rolling hills and gardens filled with flowers and decorative grasses (our favorite is called Morning Light). In the final Heaven we will see everything that exists in this world, only it will be much better and getting better all the time.

I offer a personal commentary on pets in Heaven: in our marriage, Kris and I have had four dogs: two dachshunds, a mutt, and a bichon frise. I would be very happy to share Heaven with three of the four dogs. (One of the dachshunds, Sophie, slept with us and often bit me when I got into bed.) My joy at being reunited applies especially to Webster, our happy-all-the-time bichon, who was made for Heaven. So perhaps not all dogs do go to Heaven!

I leave the last word to Joni Eareckson Tada:

Horses in heaven? Yes, I think animals are some of God's best and most avant-garde ideas; why would He throw out His greatest creative achieve-ments? . . . I'm talking about new animals fit for a new order of things. . . . [If Heaven is a new "earth" then it] just wouldn't be "earth" without animals. So, if you want to go horseback riding, meet Judy and me at the statue of the Copper Horse at the end of the bridle path in Windsor.[3]

Kris and I will be watching out the window with Webster and the other two (not three) dogs as we all frolic in Heaven's home for us. #funthingtothinkabout

Why Believe in Heaven?

A Personal Statement of Belief

For my Father's will is that everyone who looks to the Son
and believes in him shall have eternal life, and I will raise
them up at the last day.

— Jesus

The biggest question is not whether God is fair or if we'll gather with members of our earthly families, but why we should believe in Heaven itself. There are convincing reasons that should be examined, and I will give you nine of them.

The first three are reasons why Christians believe in Heaven. Following those, we will turn to some of the reasons why humans generally have believed in Heaven. Plenty of folks today poke fun at someone who believes in Heaven. I grew up with the exuberant singing of "When the roll is called up yonder, I'll be there." But for many people, that kind of talk is nonsensical or a colossal distraction from what matters most: the here and now. But I counter: either there is roll call up yonder or there is not. Either there is or there is not a Heaven in the eternal future. We can state this more forcefully: Christianity stands or falls with the resurrection of Jesus, and if resurrection teaches us anything, it teaches us that death will not have the final word and that life, eternal life with God in Heaven, is the final word.

Here then are my reasons for believing in Heaven.

Because Jesus and the Apostles Did

People of no faith tend to respect the religious genius, and certainly no one disputes that Jesus fits into the respectable religious genius camp. No one can learn about Jesus—what he said, what he did, what he believed—without knowing that he not only believed in the afterlife but also warned people, especially the corrupt religious leaders of his day, about a judgment in eternity.* One man approached Jesus and asked, "What good thing must I do to get eternal life?"† Whether or not we like what Jesus told the man—to sell all his possessions and give to the poor—Jesus affirmed the man's orientation toward Heaven. He let the man know, even in the midst of his disappointment at Jesus's answer, that if he chose he could "have treasure in heaven."

In one of Jesus's most famous parables, the parable of the sheep and goats, he pointed out that the way a person responded to "the least of these brothers and sisters of mine" would determine whether the person would enter into "eternal life." One more from Jesus: "For my Father's will is that everyone who looks to the Son and believes in him shall have eternal life, and I will raise them up at the last day."

Jesus clearly believed in the afterlife, which he called at times "eternal life" and at other times "heaven." We could nuance this quite a bit, because eternal life for Jesus begins in the here and now since the kingdom of God has been unleashed. Thus, more often than not, Jesus is talking about the final Heaven, the kingdom of God, the new Heavens and the new earth. But for now we are satisfied: Jesus believed in Heaven.

And so did the apostles.‡ Paul, for instance, when talking about this frail body of ours, said, "For we know that if the earthly tent we live in is destroyed, we have a building from God, an eternal house in heaven, not built by human hands." He told

---

* The following quotations from Jesus are from Matthew 19:16, 21; 25:31–46; John 6:40; 17:2–3; 14:1–3.
† In Matthew 19:1–24, Jesus uses a number of terms that overlap in meaning but each conveying a belief in the Age to Come as Heaven: "eternal life," "life," "heaven," and "the kingdom of heaven" and "kingdom of God".
‡ The quotations from the apostles are from 2 Corinthians 5:1; Titus 1:2; 2 Peter 1:11; 1 John 2:25.

one of his close associates, Titus, that he had a faith and knowledge resting on "the hope of eternal life." Peter, too, believed in eternal life. He promised his churches that they would "receive a rich welcome into the eternal kingdom of our Lord and Savior Jesus Christ." John said: "And this is what [God] promised us—eternal life." To be sure, "eternal life" is qualitative: it is something about the life of God entering into us now, but this qualitative eternal life that we know now is not the whole story. For John, eternal life is also quantitative, that is, it is endless and forever—in short, Heaven or the kingdom of God.

Why then do I believe in Heaven? First, because Jesus and the apostles believed in Heaven. (I'm not ashamed to say they know more than I do, and neither am I ashamed that if it was good enough for them it is good enough for me.)

Because Jesus Was Raised from the Dead

This reason is bigger than the previous one: the reality of Jesus's actual, bodily resurrection. He came back from death, others touched him, and he ate food with the disciples. All of this makes Heaven far more reasonable than anything else that is said in the Bible, and anything else that was believed by the apostles.

Because the Bible Does

A third reason for believing in Heaven—because the Bible does—might sound redundant, but there's a little more here than we found in the first reason. There's a story here, and it is one that many of us have to get a bit used to. The four simple facts are these:

Fact 1: The Old Testament shows very little interest in any kind of heaven or the afterlife.

Fact 2: The Old Testament speaks of death—*sheol*—the way other ancient Near Eastern and Mediterranean cultures did, and that means that death seems to be a permanent condition.

Fact 3: The Old Testament's only statements about the afterlife are found in the latest books in the Old Testament.

Fact 4: The New Testament ushers us into an almost brand-new hope for
      eternal life and belief in an eternal Heaven.

It would take a book (or two!), and lots of patient readers, to work through this topic carefully. We won't attempt that here. Instead, we need to see that *the Bible's major themes develop and grow and expand and take us to the very precipice of eternity.* It's like a play—say *Les Misérables*—where the whole story isn't clear until the end. It's also like a great sports contest, the World Cup or the World Series or the Super Bowl or playoff holes in a major golf tournament, where we sit on the edges of our seats and the outcome is not determined until the final moments. That is how the Bible works out the Heaven theme: all we get in most of the Old Testament, at least until Daniel's prophecies, is death in the sometimes gloomy and sometimes hopeful shady *sheol* (what the Greeks called *hades*).

But by the time Jesus comes around and by the time the apostles close the curtain of their teachings, *sheol* is a lost memory that has been swallowed up into the glorious teachings of resurrection, immortality, eternal life, and the kingdom of God. Now to be honest, Jesus didn't invent resurrection—that view was held centuries before him and grew into a strong conviction among many Jews. But a reader sensitive to developments in plots and themes can experience how hopeful the Bible becomes, from the rather gloomy pits of *sheol* to the glories of the new Heavens and the new earth. A good reason to believe in Heaven, then, is because the Bible's story leads us to believe in Heaven as the ultimate goal God has for all creation.

Because the Church Always Has

I recently read two books about Heaven called *A History of Heaven* and *Paradise Mislaid: How We Lost Heaven and How We Can Regain It.* Both were written by a Christian thinker named Jeffrey Burton Russell. The problem is that he stopped the first book in the thirteenth century with the incredibly wonderful (and annoying!) book of Dante, called *The Divine Comedy.* Then he mostly skipped three centuries and started at the same fast pace through history to our own day in his next book. When I was done with Russell, I grabbed from my shelf Gary Scott Smith's richly detailed study of how Americans have understood Heaven—from the Puritans to two great preachers, Jonathan Edwards and George Whitefield. One after another, Christian leaders, writers, preachers, and theologians talked about Heaven. There is, without question, a history of Heaven that is a history about how Christians think about Heaven.[1]

While there are two major themes in this history, the one undeniable and nonnegotiable fact is that *the church has always had a Heaven hope.* Those two themes are that Heaven is mostly a magnificent worship service or mostly a new creation society. Both themes are on target, but we want merely to point out that a good reason to believe in Heaven is that the whole church has always believed in Heaven, even as its beliefs shift from one end of the spectrum to the other.

To these three reasons why Christians (including myself) believe in Heaven, we can now add a few more.

BECAUSE OF BEAUTY

There is grandeur about our world that, if one is not too guarded, can sweep even the most rigorous atheist off her feet into moments of awe at what we experience. Perhaps it is the first glimpse of the Grand Canyon or a moment's glimpse of the Alps from an airplane. I speak personally: As a college student I participated in a missions event in Austria. When we flew over the Alps, I had a window seat. At one point the clouds broke. Snowcapped mountains came into full view with the glories of a blue sky behind them. I was overwhelmed with this world.

Perhaps for you it is a flower or a redwood forest or the music of colors or shapes or sounds brought into breathtaking harmony—think Monet or Van Gogh or Bach or Handel—or the mystery of life in the birth of a baby or a worship service with others and the sheer glory of romance and love . . .

Romanticism and Transcendentalism are seen by Christian thinkers as incomplete philosophies, but only because they make God's goods—beauty and nature—divine, instead of windows onto the divine. Those thinkers pointed us in the right direction for they saw in nature something far more than what was on the surface. Christian theologians, like Alexander Schmemann, push us to see even more in what strikes us as beautiful: God, Schmemann once said, "makes all creation the sign and means of His presence and wisdom, love, and revelation: 'O taste and see that the Lord is good.'"[2]

Most of us have had our awestruck experiences when we saw through what we saw into the beyond. But we also see the wrecks of the universe and the ravages of corruption and things gone awry. We wonder if God wants the world to continue to exist as a great place with problems, or if God wants the world eventually to be completely right. In other words, many of us believe in Heaven because we see in the present world a glimpse of something far grander: the world as what we think it ought to be. Where, I ask, do we get this sense of *ought*? And doesn't it indicate a future Heaven? If God made a world this good, has God not made a world where it will all be even better? I believe so.

BECAUSE MOST PEOPLE DO

The numbers are rather convincing. The Baylor Survey of Religion, one of the most accurate and authoritative studies ever of what Americans believe, discovered that 84 percent of Americans believe in some kind of heaven. Nearly seven out of ten (67 percent) said they were "absolutely sure," while 17 percent opted for "probably." Notably, two out of three Americans are reasonably certain they will go to heaven when they die. Women are more certain than men; African Americans more certain than white Americans; and southerners more certain than those who reside in the East or the West. Republicans are more certain of heaven than Democrats.[3] (There are no numbers for Cubs fans, but I have to think belief in heaven is higher among Cubs fans than, say, Yankees fans.)

The world, of course, is bigger than the United States. But if we look back into the ancient world—Egypt, Mesopotamia, Persia, Greece, and Rome—we will discover an even more widespread belief in the afterlife. In fact, some of it was downright weird (to us), but it was real (to them).

The ancient Egyptians considered the heavens above, or the genuine realty of the sky above, to be a massive (world-encompassing) celestial bird or cow or a woman. The sun and the stars rode across the belly of that celestial woman (her name was the goddess Nut, pronounced "newt"), and she consumed the celestial bodies at night and gave birth to them each morning.[4] Yes, it all sounds a bit weird (to us), but the bigger point must be kept in mind: the ancients all believed in the afterlife, even if they struggled mightily to make sense of it all.

If we scan the beliefs of humans across history and across the spectrum of religions and philosophies, we discover that humans have always believed in an afterlife. And most humans, at least from about the sixth century before Christ, believed in a kind of Heaven where humans will go when they die and live forever.

We are entitled, if not required, to ask these questions: Why have humans believed in Heaven? What gives rise to such beliefs across the spectrum? Does not the widespread belief in Heaven, not ignoring the occasional Ebenezer Scrooge, indicate something inherent to humans—say a gift or innate intuition from God—that there is an afterlife? How did this belief arise? The answer is almost certainly not philosophical thinking, though it played its part. The history of human belief in Heaven is an argument for believing in Heaven.

BECAUSE OF DESIRE

Nearly everyone I know believes the intense desire by teenagers to find someone to love, which often enough leads to a decade or more of searching for their soul mate, indicates that we are born to love others and born to be loved. There are just too many of us in the world with the longing to love and to be loved for this to be accidental.

C. S. Lewis takes this one step further: he observed that "if we are made for heaven, the desire for our proper place will be already in us." This "desire for our own far-off country" is a "desire which no natural happiness will satisfy."[5] Or as he put it in another context, "If I find in myself a desire which no experience in this world can satisfy, the most probable explanation is that I was made for another world."[6] American evangelical philosopher Jerry Walls wrote much the same: "A good God would not create us with the kind of aspirations we have and then leave those aspirations unsatisfied."[7]

This desire drives humans to pursue deep satisfactions and enthralling joys and answers to profound questions. Lewis said someday "the door on which we have been knocking all our lives will open at last."[8] Lewis believed our desiring leads us to Heaven. How does this indicate Heaven exists? Consider it from this perspective: Why do we want more? Why do we expect so much from our shopping for clothing or toys or technology or a new home or a better job or, most important, from the one we love the most? Most of us will admit that at times we almost bank on some person or, truth be told, a new possession to fulfill us—to make us happy. Yet why do the pleasures we desire so much last only for a short time?

Some believe—I am in their number—that the ongoing lack of fulfillment in possessing what we desire—love of another, family, beauty, work—indicates there is a true home and true North Star which, when we arrive, will fully satisfy all our desires. All the ordinary pleasures of this life that do not satisfy are gentle reminders from God that what fleetingly satisfies our desires now are promptings for a final and lasting satisfaction of the desire of all desiring: Heaven. I believe in Heaven because of desire.

BECAUSE OF JUSTICE

Probably the most important reason many people believe in Heaven, or at least want there to be a Heaven, is because of justice. Better yet, because of injustice. I've heard my whole life that "Life isn't fair," and that's very true. But why do I rise up in protest against this commonplace line whenever I see small children with bloated bellies or children left unloved rolling monotonously in beds in underprovided orphanages? Or when I hear of really good candidates for a job who are ousted because someone's relative also applied? Or when a gifted young person is deprived of a dream for further education because a father died and a mother needs that young adult to work to make ends meet? Or a young person who cannot find love with another because of a violation that happened years before in the darkness of night? I rise up, and so do you, because we detest the ruins of injustices.

I believe in Heaven because I believe God wants to make all things right. Because God wants justice finally to be known and established. That means those who have experienced the horrors of injustices will someday sit under the shade tree of justice and know that God makes all things new, so new that past injustices are swallowed up in the joy of new creation. I believe in Heaven because I believe in a final and lasting justice.

BECAUSE SCIENCE DOESN'T PROVIDE ALL THE ANSWERS

Science tells us only what science can tell us—how the world works and behaves as it does. It can probe age and origins, but it cannot probe meaning and purpose. A famous statement by astronomer Robert Jastrow is a fitting conclusion to our reasons for why we believe in Heaven.

> For the scientist who has lived by his faith in the power of reason, the story ends like a bad dream. He has scaled the mountains of ignorance; he is about to conquer the highest peak; as he pulls himself over the final rock, he is greeted by a band of theologians who have been sitting there for centuries.[9]

The apostles are in the center of those theologians, but rising tall above them and over them all is Jesus, the One who was raised. He explains it all to the scientists who will listen. He reveals to them a dream with a fulfillment that is beyond what their dreams could ever anticipate.

After Words

I cannot say enough about the collegial and supporting environment I have found at Northern Seminary, so my thanks to the Board and to Alistair Brown, Karen Walker-Freeburg, and my colleagues and students. Among our students none stands out for me more than Tara Beth Leach who not only is my graduate assistant but also became a conversation partner in all things about Heaven. I am also grateful to friends who have read the manuscript or parts of it, including Dan Kimball, Ed Noble, Andy Stanley, Rick Warren, Andy McQuitty, and Doug Halsne.

My literary agent, Greg Daniel, not only suggested this topic to me over breakfast one day at Egg Harbor in Libertyville, but has also handled this project with enthusiasm and expertise.

Kris, my wife, has once again endured another immersion in a new topic. She read and made detailed comments on the entire manuscript and has made the book better in every way imaginable.

Notes

Chapter 1: Surprising Places

1. This story has been told by many, but a good sketch is Eberhard Bethge, *Dietrich Bonhoeffer: A Biography,* rev. ed. (Minneapolis: Fortress, 2000), 38. Perhaps more revealing is the little sketch by Bonhoeffer himself of his childhood fears: Dietrich Bonhoeffer, *Dietrich Bonhoeffer: Ecumenical, Academic, and Pastoral Work: 1932–1932,* ed. Eberhard Amerlun et al., Dietrich Bonhoeffer Works 11 (Minneapolis: Fortress, 2012), 396–97.

2. Carol Zaleski and Philip Zaleski, eds., *The Book of Heaven: An Anthology of Writings from Ancient to Modern Times* (New York: Oxford University Press, 2000), 288–91.

3. Julian Barnes, *A History of the World in 10 1/2 Chapters* (New York: Vintage Books, 1990), 283–97, 298–99.

4. See Jerry L. Walls, *Heaven: The Logic of Eternal Joy* (New York: Oxford University Press, 2002), 14–15.

5. Karen Spears Zacharias, "Notes from Mama's Bible," *Karen Spears Zacharias* (blog), June 26, 2013, http://karenzach.com/notes-from-mamas-bible/.

6. Ernest Hemingway, *Selected Letters 1917–1961,* ed. Carlos Baker (New York: First Scribner Classics Edition, 2003), 165–66.

7. Ann O'Neill, "The Reinvention of Ted Turner," CNN, November 17, 2013, www.cnn.com/2013/11/17/us/ted-turner-profile/.

8. These options are discussed clearly in Arthur O. Roberts, *Exploring Heaven: What Great Christian Thinkers Tell Us About Our Afterlife with God* (San Francisco: HarperSanFrancisco, 2003), 12–34.

Chapter 2: Imaginations of the Imaginative

1. "The Apostles' Creed," Creeds.net, www.creeds.net/ancient/apostles.htm#Modern; "The Nicene Creed," Creeds.net, www.creeds.net/ancient/nicene.htm.

2. "Westminster Confession of Faith," The Constitution of the Presbyterian Church in the United States of America (Columbia University, 1986), 136. www.reformed.org/documents/wcf_with_proofs/.

3. There are many good books on heaven in history, including these: Jeffrey Burton Russell, *A History of Heaven* (Princeton, NJ: Princeton University Press, 1998); Jeffrey Burton

Russell, *Paradise Mislaid: How We Lost Heaven and How We Can Regain It* (New York: Oxford University Press, 2006); Colleen McDannell and Bernhard Lang, *Heaven: A History* (New Haven: Yale University Press, 1995); Gary Scott Smith, *Heaven in the American Imagination* (New York: Oxford University Press, 2011); Alister E. McGrath, *A Brief History of Heaven,* Blackwell's Brief Histories of Religion (Oxford: Blackwell, 2003).

4. Mark Twain, *Tom Sawyer and Huckleberry Finn* (New York: Alfred A. Knopf, 1991), 239.

5. Arthur O. Roberts, *Exploring Heaven: What Great Christian Thinkers Tell Us About Our Afterlife with God* (San Francisco: HarperSanFrancisco, 2003), 114.

6. A. W. Tozer, *Whatever Happened to Worship* (Camp Hill, PA: WingSpread, 2012), 13.

7. William J. Peterson, *Martin Luther Had a Wife* (Wheaton: Tyndale, 1983), 20–21. For more on Katie (Katharina von Bora), see Kirsi Stjerna, *Women and the Reformation* (Oxford: Blackwell, 2009), 51–70.

8. Armin Stein, *Katharine von Bora: Dr. Martin Luther's Wife* (n.p.: General Council Publication Board, 1915), 40–78, 159, eBook; Stjerna, *Women and the Reformation.*

Chapter 3: Heaven, It's a Promise!

1. Billy Graham, "Remarks by Dr. Billy Graham at Richard Nixon's Funeral," Watergate. info, April 27, 1994, http://watergate.info/1994/04/27/billy-graham-remarks-at-nixon -funeral.html.

2. Graham, "Remarks by Dr. Billy Graham at Richard Nixon's Funeral."

3. Herbert Lockyer, *All the Promises of the Bible* (Grand Rapids: Zondervan, 1990), front cover.

Chapter 4: The Heart of the Promise

1. Sam Bisbee, *You're Telling Me,* 1934, Paramount Pictures, www.imdb.com/title /tt0026017/?ref_=fn_al_tt_3.

2. W. Somerset Maugham, quoted in Robin Maugham, *Conversations with Willie: Recollections of W. Somerset Maugham* (New York: Simon and Schuster, 1978), 6.

3. Woody Allen, "Death, A Play," in *Without Feathers* (New York: Random House, 1975), 99.

4. C. S. Lewis, *A Grief Observed* (New York: HarperOne, 2009), 17.

5. Lewis, *A Grief Observed,* 18.

6. Lewis, *A Grief Observed,* 28, 37, 66.

7. Malcolm Muggeridge, *Chronicles of Wasted Time: An Autobiography* (Vancouver: Regent College Publishing, 2006), 32.

8. N. T. Wright, *Surprised by Hope: Rethinking Heaven, the Resurrection, and the Mission of the Church* (New York: HarperOne, 2008), xiii–xiv.

9. Lisa Miller, *Heaven: Our Enduring Fascination with the Afterlife* (New York: Harper, 2010), 107.

10. Wright, *Surprised by Hope,* 63.

Chapter 5: The Christian Belief

1. Chris Spielman, *That's Why I'm Here: The Chris and Stefanie Spielman Story* (Grand Rapids: Zondervan, 2012).

2. Siddhartha Mukherjee, *The Emperor of All Maladies: A Biography of Cancer* (New York: Scribner, 2010).

3. Spielman, *That's Why I'm Here,* 181.

4. Spielman, *That's Why I'm Here,* 182, 208.

5. Two very important books on the Jewish view of the resurrection, both by Jewish scholars, are: Alan F. Segal, *Life After Death: A History of the Afterlife in Western Religion* (New York: Doubleday, 2004); Jon D. Levenson, *Resurrection and the Restoration of Israel: The Ultimate Victory of the God of Life* (New Haven: Yale University Press, 2008).

6. N. T. Wright, *The Resurrection of the Son of God,* The New Testament and the Question of God 3 (Minneapolis: Fortress, 2003), 86.

7. Josh Ross, *Scarred Faith: This Is a Story About How Honesty, Grief, a Cursing Toddler, Risk-Taking, AIDS, Hope, Brokenness, Doubts, and Memphis Ignited Adventurous Faith* (New York: Howard Books, 2013), 18–19, 25, 29, 30–31.

8. Ross, *Scarred Faith,* 33.

9. Spielman, *That's Why I'm Here,* 169.

10. Sharon van der Walde, review, "The Best Book I've Read in a Very Long Time," Amazon. com, April 27, 2012, www.amazon.com/Thats-Why-Im-Here-Stefanie/dp/0310336147 /ref=sr_1_1?ie=UTF8&qid=1428512936&sr=8-1&keywords=that%27s+why+i%27m +here+spielman.

11. C. S. Lewis, *The Lion, the Witch and the Wardrobe* (New York: HarperCollins, 2003), 93–94.

Chapter 6: Heaven: In Heaven or on Earth?

1. Alessandro Scafi, *Maps of Paradise* (Chicago: University of Chicago, 2013), 11.

2. For an image: http://upload.wikimedia.org/wikipedia/commons/3/39/Ebstorfer -stich2.jpg.

3. Scafi, *Maps of Paradise,* 72.

4. See the diagram on page 42 in Colleen McDannell and Bernhard Lang, *Heaven: A History* (New Haven: Yale University Press, 1988).

5. N. T. Wright, *Surprised by Scripture: Engaging Contemporary Issues* (New York: HarperOne, 2014), 96–97.

6. Randy Alcorn, *Heaven* (Wheaton, IL: Tyndale, 2004), 42.

7. J. R. R. Tolkien, "Leaf by Niggle," *Tree and Leaf,* 100–107, 113, heroicjourneys.files. wordpress.com/2008/09/niggle.pdf.

Chapter 7: Facing Death Standing in the Empty Tomb

1. Dietrich Bonhoeffer, *Letters and Papers from Prison,* ed. John W. de Gruchy, Dietrich Bonhoeffer Works, vol. 8 (Minneapolis: Fortress, 2010), 322.

2. I adapted this from the list in Herbert Lockyer, *Last Words of Saints and Sinners* (Grand Rapids: Kregel, 1969), 43.

3. The following story is told in a number of studies. See Eberhard Bethge, *Dietrich Bonhoeffer: A Biography,* rev. ed. (Minneapolis: Fortress, 2000), 918–28.

4. Christian Wiman, *My Bright Abyss: Meditation of a Modern Believer* (New York: Farrar, Staus and Giroux, 2013), 33, 34, 37.

5. Larissa Heatley, "Give 'Em Heaven," *The High Calling (blog),* www.thehighcalling.org /family/give-em-heaven#.Ua-Ip5Xvz7f.

6. Gary Black Jr., *Preparing for Heaven* (New York: HarperOne, 2015), forthcoming, with permission of author.

7. Henry D. Rack, *Reasonable Enthusiast: John Wesley and the Rise of Methodism,* 2nd ed. (Nashville: Abingdon, 1993), 532.

8. J. Wilbur Chapman, *The Life and Work of Dwight Lyman Moody* (Chicago: Moody Press, 2012), www.biblebelievers.com/moody/27.html.

9. Leo van Noppen, *The Critical Reception of Gerard Manley Hopkins in the Netherlands and Flanders, 1908–1979* (Waterloo, Ontario: International Hopkins Association, 1980), n.p.

10. Eric Metaxas, *Amazing Grace: William Wilberforce and the Heroic Campaign to End Slavery* (New York: HarperOne, 2007), 275.

Chapter 8: The First Promise: God Will Be God

1. Gary Scott Smith, *Heaven in the American Imagination* (New York: Oxford University Press, 2011), vii, reformatted as a numbered list.

2. Jeffrey Burton Russell, *A History of Heaven* (Princeton, NJ: Princeton University Press, 1997), 143.

3. Kieran Kavanaugh, ed., *John of the Cross: Selected Writings*, The Classics of Western Spirituality (New York: Paulist Press, 1987), 285.

4. John Henry Newman quoted in Carol Zaleski and Philip Zaleski, eds., *The Book of Heaven: An Anthology of Writings from Ancient to Modern Times* (New York: Oxford University Press, 2000), 198.

5. Colleen McDannell and Bernhard Lang, *Heaven: A History* (New Haven: Yale University Press, 1988), 59.

6. J. I. Packer, *Concise Theology* (Wheaton, IL: Tyndale, 1993), 267.

7. Richard J. Foster, *Prayer: Finding the Heart's True Home* (San Francisco: HarperSanFrancisco, 1992), 161–62.

Chapter 9: The Second Promise: Jesus Will Be Jesus

1. C. S. Lewis, *Essay Collection: Faith, Christianity and the Church*, ed. L. Walmsley (London: HarperCollins, 2000), 100.

2. Chris Tomlin, Ed Cash, Jesse Reeves, "How Great Is Our God," *Arriving*, copyright © 2004, Alletrop Music (BMI).

3. Malcolm Muggeridge, *Chronicles of Wasted Time: An Autobiography* (Vancouver: Regent College Publishing, 2006), 232, emphasis added.

4. Muggeridge, *Chronicles of Wasted Time*, 232.

Chapter 10: The Third Promise: Heaven Will Be the Utopia of Pleasures

1. Darrin M. McMahon, *Happiness: A History* (New York: Atlantic Monthly Press, 2006), xii.

2. St. Augustine, quoted in Scot McKnight, *Kingdom Conspiracy: Returning to the Radical Mission of the Local Church* (Grand Rapids: Brazos, 2014), 203.

3. Stewart Goetz, *The Purpose of Life: A Theistic Perspective* (London/New York: Continuum, 2012), 10.

4. Lewis, quoted in Goetz, *Purpose of Life*, 11–12.

5. Lewis, quoted in Goetz, *Purpose of Life*, 12.

6. Eric J. Gilchrest, "Jewish Utopia," chap. 3 in *Revelation 21–22 in Light of Jewish and Greco-Roman Utopianism*, Biblical Interpretation Series 118 (Leiden/Boston: Brill, 2013).

7. Jonathan Edwards, *The Works of Jonathan Edwards*, vol. 2 (W. Ball, 1839), 901, Google eBook.

8. C. S. Lewis, *The Last Battle* (New York: HarperCollins, 2002), 228.

Chapter 11: The Fourth Promise: Heaven Will Be Eternal Life

1. I sketch this story in two of my books, and it is reduced here to focus on one important theme: the final heaven as the renewed world and our calling to be image-bearers in that final heaven. See Scot McKnight, *The King Jesus Gospel: The Original Good News Revisited* (Grand Rapids: Zondervan, 2011); Scot McKnight, *Kingdom Conspiracy: Returning to the Radical Mission of the Local Church* (Grand Rapids: Brazos, 2014). For a recent sketch from a different angle, one that emphasizes our cultural calling, see J. Richard Middleton, *A New Heaven and a New Earth: Reclaiming Biblical Eschatology* (Grand Rapids: BakerAcademic, 2014), 37–73.

2. Zaleski, *The Book of Heaven*, 217.

3. Miron Dolot, *Execution by Hunger: The Hidden Holocaust* (New York: W. W. Norton, 1985).

4. The Guttmacher Institute, "Facts on Induced Abortion in the United States," February 2014, www.guttmacher.org/pubs/fb_induced_abortion.html.

5. Amnesty International, "Culture of Discrimination: A Fact Sheet on 'Honor' Killings," 2012, http://webcache.googleusercontent.com/search?q=cache:E9BHGNGAGgEJ :www.amnestyusa.org/sites/default/files/pdfs/honor_killings_fact_sheet_final_2012 .doc+&cd=2&hl=en&ct=clnk&gl=us.

6. Mukherjee, *The Emperor of All Maladies*, xi.

7. Bree Loverly, "Zekey Is Finally Home, *Bree Loverly* (blog), March 24, 2014, http:// breeloverly.com/2014/03/zekey-is-finally-home/. Used with permission.

8. Andy Holt, "Zeke Has Gone Home," *The Sometimes Preacher* (blog), March 23, 2014, http://thesometimespreacher.com/2014/03/zeke-has-gone-home/. Used with permission.

9. Holt, "The Reason for Our Hope," *The Sometimes Preacher* (blog), http:// thesometimespreacher.com/2014/06/the-reason-for-our-hope/. Used with permission.

Chapter 12: The Fifth Promise: Heaven Will Be an Eternal Global Fellowship

1. Willa Cather, *O Pioneers!* (Boston: Houghton Mifflin, 1913), 122.

2. Cather, *O Pioneers!* 122–23.

3. These have been expertly sketched by Alister E. McGrath, *A Brief History of Heaven*, Blackwell's Brief Histories of Religion (Oxford: Blackwell, 2003), 6.

4. Nigel Dixon, *Villages Without Walls: An Exploration of the Necessity of Building Christian Community in a Post-Christian World* (Palmerston North, New Zealand: Vox Humana, 2010), 54–62.

5. David Foster Wallace, *A Supposedly Fun Thing I'll Never Do Again* (New York: Back Bay Books, 1997), 38.

6. George Eliot, *Scenes of a Clerical Life* (New York: Penguin Classics, 1999), 74.

7. Eugene Peterson, *Living the Resurrection: The Risen Christ in Everyday Life* (Colorado Springs: NavPress, 2006), 65.

8. Peterson, *Living the Resurrection*, 71.

9. A wonderful sketch of weddings among first-century Jews, including menu and recipes, can be found in Douglas E. Neel and Joel A. Pugh, *The Food and Feasts of Jesus: Inside the World of First-Century Fare, With Menus and Recipes*, Religion in the Modern World (Lanham, MD: Rowman and Littlefield, 2012), 115–39.

10. Richard J. Mouw, *When the Kings Come Marching In: Isaiah and the New Jerusalem*, rev. ed. (Grand Rapids: Wm. B. Eerdmans, 2002), 97.

11. Scot McKnight, *A Fellowship of Differents: Showing the World God's Design for Life Together* (Grand Rapids: Zondervan, 2015).

12. Peter Kreeft, *Everything You Wanted to Know about Heaven, But Never Dreamed of Asking!* (San Francisco: Ignatius Press, 1990), 80, emphasis in original.

13. Taken from my eBook, *Junia Is Not Alone*.

14. eBook, *Junia Is Not Alone*.

15. L. C. Warner, *Saving Women: Retrieving Evangelistic Theology and Practice* (Waco, TX: Baylor University Press, 2007).

16. Zaleski, *The Book of Heaven*, 377.

Chapter 13: The Sixth Promise: Heaven Will Be an Eternal Beloved Community

1. Mouw, *When the Kings Come Marching In*, 39, 57.

2. Kreeft, *Every Thing You Wanted to Know about Heaven*, 79.

3. Petronius, *The Satyricon*, chap. 28–36, Gutenberg.org, www.gutenberg.org/ebooks /5225.

4. Jennifer Wehunt, "The Food Desert," *Chicago Magazine*, August 11, 2009, www .chicagomag.com/Chicago-Magazine/July-2009/The-Food-Desert/.

5. Stanley Ratliff, *A Dream, A Goal, Never a Reality: A True Story of Superior Movement* (Bloomington, IN: AuthorHouse, 2008).

6. Ratliff, *A Dream, A Goal*.

7. Wayne Gordon, *Real Hope in Chicago: The Incredible Story of How the Gospel Is Transforming a Chicago Neighborhood* (Grand Rapids: Zondervan, 1995), 31.

8. Gordon, *Real Hope in Chicago*, 32–33.

Chapter 14: The First Hour in Heaven

1. Mouw, *When the Kings Come Marching In*, 60.
2. Leslie Leyland Fields and Dr. Jill Hubbard, *Forgiving Our Fathers and Mothers: Finding Freedom from Hurt and Hate* (Nashville: W, 2014), xvii–xviii, 31–32, 110, 181, 162.
3. Marilynne Robinson, *Gilead* (New York: Farrar, Straus, Giroux, 2004), 57.
4. Miroslav Volf, *The End of Memory: Remembering Rightly in a Violent World* (Grand Rapids: Wm. B. Eerdmans, 2006), 17.
5. Volf, *The End of Memory*, 96–102.
6. Mitch Albom, *The Five People You Meet in Heaven* (New York: Hyperion, 2003), 35.

Chapter 15: How Should Heaven People Live Today?

1. Gary Scott Smith, *Heaven in the American Imagination* (New York: Oxford University Press, 2011), 193.
2. "This World Is Not My Home," Writers: Mary Reeves Davis and Albert E. Brumley, Copyright 1965, Sony/ATV Tree Publishing.
3. Harry Emerson Fosdick, *The Assurance of Immortality* (New York: Association Press, 1918), 6.
4. Charles Reynolds Brown, *A Working Faith*, quoted in Smith, *Heaven*, 139.
5. C. S. Lewis, *Mere Christianity* (New York: Zondervan, 1952), 134.
6. Eugene Peterson, *Living the Resurrection: The Risen Christ in Everyday Life* (Colorado Springs: NavPress, 2006), 67.
7. Joseph M. Stowell, *Eternity: Reclaiming a Passion for What Endures* (Chicago: Moody Press, 1995), 98–110.
8. Timothy Williamson, "How Can Imagination Change the World?" Big Questions Online, June 25, 2013, www.bigquestionsonline.com/content/how-can-imagination-change-world.
9. James D. G. Dunn, *The Acts of the Apostles*, Narrative Commentaries (Valley Forge, PA: Trinity, 1996), 12.
10. I borrow these four categories from John R. Levison, *Inspired: The Holy Spirit and the Mind of Faith* (Grand Rapids: Wm. B. Eerdmans, 2013), 201–9.
11. Dietrich Bonhoeffer, "Meditation on Psalm 119," *Theological Education Underground: 1937-1940*, ed. Dirk Schulz and Victoria J. Barnett, Dietrich Bonhoeffer Works 15 (Minneapolis: Fortress, 2012), 522.
12. Martin Luther, quoted in David Goh, *Blueprint for Greater Success* (New Delhi: Sterling, 2000), 121.
13. Elizabeth Achtemeier, *Not Til I Have Done: A Personal Testimony* (Louisville: Westminster John Knox, 1999), 33.

14. C. S. Lewis, *The Great Divorce: A Dream* (New York: HarperCollins, 2001), 75.

15. Fields, *Forgiving Our Fathers and Mothers,* 188.

16. Fields, *Forgiving Our Fathers and Mothers,* 128.

17. Fields, *Forgiving Our Fathers and Mothers,* 149–50.

18. Fields, *Forgiving Our Fathers and Mothers,* 150.

19. Brennan Manning, *All Is Grace: A Ragamuffin Memoir* (Colorado Springs: David C. Cook, 2011), 31.

20. Manning, *All Is Grace: A Ragamuffin Memoir,* 51, 71, 107.

21. Manning, *All Is Grace: A Ragamuffin Memoir,* 176.

22. Manning, *All Is Grace: A Ragamuffin Memoir,* 196.

Chapter 16: What About Near-Death Experiences?

1. Anil Seth, "Near-Death Experiences: The Brain's Last Hurrah?" *Guardian,* August 15, 2003, www.bbc.com/news/science-environment-23672150.

2. Arthur O. Roberts, *Exploring Heaven: What Great Christian Thinkers Tell Us About Our Afterlife with God* (San Francisco: HarperSanFrancisco, 2003), 70.

3. Jerry L. Walls, *Heaven: The Logic of Eternal Joy* (New York: Oxford University Press, 2002), 160.

4. Mally Cox-Chapman, *The Case for Heaven: Near-Death Experiences as Evidence of the Afterlife* (New York: G. P. Putnam's Sons, 1995), 2, 6, 10, 23, 58. For another and more expansive summary, see Jeffrey Burton Russell, *A History of Heaven* (Princeton, NJ: Princeton University Press, 1997), 111–12.

5. Lisa Miller, *Heaven: Our Enduring Fascination with the Afterlife* (New York: Harper, 2010), 217.

6. Cox-Chapman, *The Case for Heaven,* 162, 176.

7. Carol Zaleski, *Otherworld Journeys: Accounts of Near-Death Experience in Medieval and Modern Times* (New York: Oxford University Press, 1987), 188–90.

8. Zaleski, *Otherworld Journeys,* 190.

9. Zaleski, *The Book of Heaven,* 60–66, 111–15.

10. Dan Ben-Amos and Jerome R. Mintz, eds., *In Praise of the Baal Shem Tov: The Earliest Collection of Legends about the Founder of Hasidism* (Northvale, NJ: Jason Aronson, 1993), 4.

11. James L. Garlow and Keith Wall, *Heaven and the Afterlife* (Minneapolis: Bethany House, 2009) , 267–74.

Chapter 17: What About Rewards in Heaven?

1. Kreeft, *Every Thing You Wanted to Know About Heaven,* 29.

2. Ezra Stiles, *A Sermon Delivered at the Ordination of the Reverend Henry Channing* (New London, CT: T. Green, 1787), 39–40, quoted in Gary Scott Smith, *Heaven in the American Imagination* (New York: Oxford University Press, 2011), 56.

3. R. T. France, *The Gospel of Matthew,* New International Commentary on the New Testament (Grand Rapids: Wm. B. Eerdmans, 2007), 748.

4. For a defense of this view, see Craig L. Blomberg, "Degrees of Reward in the Kingdom of Heaven?" *Journal of the Evangelical Theological Society* 35 (1992): 159–72.

Chapter 18: Who Will Be in Heaven?

1. "Revelation," in Flannery O'Connor, *The Complete Stories* (New York: Farrar, Straus and Giroux, 1971), 488–509.

2. Catherine A. Brekus, *Sarah Osborn's World: The Rise of Evangelical Christianity in Early America* (New Haven: Yale University Press, 2013), 87.

3. For example, John R. W. Stott and David L. Edwards, *Evangelical Essentials: A Liberal-Evangelical Dialogue* (Downers Grove, IL: IVP, 1988), 327.

4. From the Ch'u Tz'u, traced to Ch'ü Yüan, lines 32–37, quoted in Zaleski and Zaleski, *The Book of Heaven,* 56.

5. Kreeft, *Everything You Always Wanted to Know About Heaven,* 243.

6. Max Lucado, *Beyond Heaven's Door* (Nashville: Thomas Nelson, 2013), 25–26.

7. Kreeft, *Everything You Always Wanted to Know About Heaven,* 248–49.

Chapter 19: Is God Fair?

1. Jerry L. Walls, *Heaven: The Logic of Eternal Joy* (New York: Oxford University Press, 2002), 63–91, especially 66–67.

Chapter 20: Will There Be Families?

1. Randy Alcorn, *Touchpoints: Heaven* (Carol Stream, Illinois: Tyndale, 2014), 105.

2. Arthur O. Roberts, *Exploring Heaven: What Great Christian Thinkers Tell Us About Our Afterlife with God* (San Francisco: HarperSanFrancisco, 2003), 126.

3. Garlow and Wall, *Heaven and the Afterlife,* 166.

4. Sheldon Vanauken, *A Severe Mercy* (San Francisco: HarperOne, 2009), 24, 43.

5. C. S. Lewis, quoted in Vanauken, *A Severe Mercy,* 93, 125.

6. Vanauken, *A Severe Mercy.*

7. Perhaps more was at work in their argument, perhaps something like this:
    Since the final resurrection will mean the resumption and perfection of life under the Law, and

Since the Torah teaches that divorce is wrong, and

  a. Since the Torah teaches that if a husband dies without a child his brother is to marry the woman to raise up a "seed" for that original husband, and

  b. Since a woman living under that that Torah had seven different brother-husbands, and

  c. Since they had all died, and

  d. Since—now I go back to the first "since"—the resurrection will resume and perfect the present life under the Law, and

  e. Since marriage is for one man and one woman according to the Law, and

  f. Since that woman had more than one husband . . .

  g. Since if she resumes marriage with her original husband she must divorce, which against the Law, or

  h. Since if she resumes marriage with all seven she'd be a polygamist. . . .

  i. *Then* doesn't a resurrection create disobedience to the Torah and an impossible life?!

8. St. Augustine, quoted in McDannell and Lang, *Heaven: A History,* 64.

Chapter 21: *What About Children Who Die?*

1. See "Infant Death," CDC, www.cdc.gov/mmwr/preview/mmwrhtml/mm4838a2.htm.

2. US Census Bureau, International Database, quoted in "Infant Mortality Rates of Countries," www.infoplease.com/ipa/A0934744.html.

3. Karen Spears Zacharias, *After the Flag Has Been Folded: A Daughter Remembers the Father She Lost to War—and the Mother Who Held Her Family Together* (New York: Harper Paperbacks, 2006), 246–63.

4. E-mail correspondence with author, February 13, 2015, used by permission.

5. Catherine A. Brekus, *Sarah Osborn's World: The Rise of Evangelical Christianity in Early America* (New Haven: Yale University Press, 2013), 137, 143, 144, 147, 149, 157, 166.

6. My favorite brief discussion is Graham Twelftree, *Life After Death,* Thinking Clearly Series (Grand Rapids: Monarch, 2002), 149–53.

7. Twelftree, *Life After Death,* 153.

Chapter 22: *What About Cremation?*

1. *Book of Common Prayer* (The Episcopal Church, 1979), 485.

2. Graham, quoted in Alister E. McGrath, *A Brief History of Heaven,* Blackwell's Brief Histories of Religion (Oxford: Blackwell, 2003), 37.

Chapter 23: What About Purgatory?

1. For a discussion of the early church and purgatory, see M. Maritano, "Purgatory," in Angelo Di Berardino, ed., *Encyclopedia of Ancient Christianity,* 2nd ed. (Downers Grove, IL: IVP Academic, 2014), 3.355; Jerry L. Walls, *Purgatory: The Logic of Total Transformation* (New York: Oxford University Press, 2012).
2. Twelftree, *Life After Death,* 152.

Chapter 24: Will There Be Pets in Heaven?

1. Mouw, *When the Kings Come Marching In,* 20–21.
2. Mouw, *When the Kings Come Marching In,* 21.
3. Joni Eareckson Tada, *Heaven, Your Real Home* (Grand Rapids: Zondervan, 1995), 55.

Chapter 25: Why Believe in Heaven?

1. Jeffrey Burton Russell, *A History of Heaven* (Princeton, NJ: Princeton University Press, 1997); Jeffrey Burton Russell, *Paradise Mislaid: How We Lost Heaven—and How We Can Regain It* (New York: Oxford University Press, 2007); Smith, *Heaven in the American Imagination.*
2. Alexander Schmemann, *For the Life of the World: Sacraments and Orthodoxy* (Crestwood, NY: St. Vladimir's Seminary Press, 2000), 14.
3. Rodney Stark, ed., *What Americans Really Believe: New Findings from the Baylor Study of Religion* (Waco, TX: Baylor University Press, 2008), 69–74.
4. J. Edward Wright, *The Early History of Heaven* (New York: Oxford University Press, 2000), 9–23.
5. C. S. Lewis, *Essay Collection: Faith, Christianity and the Church,* ed. L. Walmsley (London: HarperCollins, 2000), 98–99.
6. C. S. Lewis, *Mere Christianity* (New York: HarperCollins, 1952), 136–37.
7. Walls, *Heaven: The Logic of Eternal Joy,* 31.
8. Lewis, *Essay Collection: Faith, Christianity and the Church,* 103.
9. Robert Jastrow, *God and the Astronomers* (New York: W. W. Norton & Co., 1992), 107.